Cee Dub's
Dutch Oven
and Other Camp Cookin'

A Back Country Guide to Outdoor Cooking
Spiced with Tall Tales
Revised Edition

By C. W. "Butch" Welch

Back Country Press
Penny L. Welch, Publisher

Copyright © 1999 by C.W. "Butch" Welch

Printed in the United States
First Printing - 1996
Second Printing - 19
Third Printing - 200
Fourth Printing - 20
Fifth Printing - 200
Sixth Printing - 20
Seventh Printing - 200

Illustrations by Ellis Pendergraft
Computer Graphics - C. Robertson

ISBN # 0-9672647-1-5

DEDICATION

To Buzz and Betty, my folks, who in their own
right could be called "Good Cooks"
and
also to my three sisters
Julia, Carol, and Deborah
for their well intentioned ridicule
of that first effort at cooking dinner
which first motivated me to
become a "Good Cook".

C. W. "Butch" Welch
aka "Cee Dub"

The Old Rock House
Lake Lowell, Idaho

May 1996

_____Table of Contents_____

About the Author - An Introduction To Cee Dub 10

About the Cooks! 17

Good Cooks/Bad Cooks 18

Good Humored Cook 23

Don't Criticize the Cook... 24

Chicken Ala S@#T 26

Dutch Oven & Cast Iron Cookery 28

Camp Kitchens 31

Basic Camp Kitchen - The Check Lists 34

Gettin' Started 38

Camp Cooking with Dutch Ovens 40

    Dutch Ovens - Selection and Care 41

    Decking your Dutches 47

    Things I Don't Care to Eat 49

    Is It Done Yet? 50

    Cooking "Lite" 51

    Planning Your Menu 53

    Cooking for VIPs 54

Bread in Camp _____ 57

    Getting Bread in Camp 58

    Bread and Horse Wrecks 60

    A Pinch of This and a Dash of That 63

    Sourdough 65

    Uncle Jack's Sourdough 66

    Sourdough Hotcake Batter 67

    Sourdough Bread 68

    Cee Dub's Sourdough Biscuits 69

    Poor Man's Sourdough Pancakes 70

    Cee Dub's Basic Biscuits 71

    Angel Biscuits " Bigmama's Best" 72

    Dutch Oven Cornbread I and II 73

    Mexican Cornbread 74

    Sara'a Mexican Cornbread 75

    Camp Bread 76

    Camp French Toast 77

Meat in Camp 78

    Barbeque Texas Style 79

    Game Meat 84

Table of Contents

Meat in Camp Continued

Elk Rib or Brisket Barbeque 88
Butch's BBQ Sauce 89
Leg of Lamb or Ram 90
Lamb Shanks with Garlic 92
Elk Rosemary 93
Middle Fork Spareribs 94
Dutch Oven Barbeque Brisket 96
Barbeque Spareribs 97
Shortribs with Dumplings 98
Liver & Onions • Swiss Steak 99
Baked Elk Heart with Sage Dressing 100
Mike's Dutch Oven BBQ - Pork Rib Dinner 101
Game Warden Scramble 102

Favorite Camp Meals 103

Hearty Dutch Oven Breakfast 104
Dutch Oven Omelette 105
Garden Vegetable Eggs 106
Breakfast Meats Dutch Oven Style 107
Dutch Oven Lasagna 108
Cooking from Cans • Sandbar Pasta Salad 110
Tangy Glazed Hams • Canned Yams 111
Howard's Refried Beans 112
Kraut and Dogs 113
Elk n' Kraut 114

Fowl & Fish 115

Brother-in-Law Duck 116
Dutch Oven Wild Duck or Goose in Gravy 117
Roast Duck in a Dutch 118
Almond Duck with Mandarin Oranges 119
Hungry Ridge Chicken 120
Camp Robertson Quick-fix Chicken 122
Lib's Dutch Oven Chicken.. 124
Carlson Ranch Sage Chicken 125
Butch's Bitchin Chicken.. 126
Beck's Honey Mustard Roasted Chicken 127
Stuffed Cornish Game Hens 128
Blue Grouse Cacciatore 129

Table of Contents

Fowl & Fish Continued

Sara's Camp Chicken 130
Stream-Side Salmon 131
Scout Burger 131
Campfire Poached Fish • Frying Pan Hollandaise 132
Seviche 133
How to Cook a Coot 134

Camp Chili, Stews, Soups and Sauces 136

Chili, the Controversy and the Recipes 137
Howard's South Texas Chili 141
Cee Dub's Yankee Chili 142
Howard's Onion, Chili and Cheese Casserole 143
Chili con Carne and Beans 144
Bruneau River Green pork Chii & Enchiladas 146
Stew 148
Gospel Hump Soup 149
Camp Crockpot 150
Winter's Day Stew 152
Basic Venison Stew 153
Warden Stew 154
Steffado (Rabbit Stew) 156
Basic Soup Stock 157
Vegetable Soup 158
Fish Stock 159
Chicken/Poultry Stock 160
Chicken & Noodle & Jack Cheese Casserole 161
Trish's Talmaks Soup 162
Basco's Teriyaki • Bergman's Meat Marinade 163
Quick Meat Marinade • Cee Dub's Italian Red Sauce 164
Beer Batter • Captain Bob's Tempura Beer Batter 165
Marinated Vegetables 166
Rainbow Rice 166
Cornstarch Gravy • Sausage Gravy 167
Quick Camp White Sauce and Basic Brown Sauce 168
Homemade Cheese Sauce 170

Vegetables in Camp 171

Potatoes a/k/a Taters, Spuds 172
Quick Fried Taters • Baked Spuds River Style 173

Table of Contents

Spuds and Onions Au Gratin 174
Breakfast Taters 175
Homemade Hash 177
Homemade Hash with Wide Eyes 177
No Name Creek Baked Beans 178
Mixed Italian Vegetables • Cee Dub's Fancy Veggies 180
Easy Oriental Vegetables• Quick Fresh Mixed Veggies 181
Baked Corn Casserole • Middle Fork Mexican Corn 182
Quick & Simple Green Beans • Ranch Veggies 183
Cauliflower & Broccolli with Pepper Cheese
     Sauce•Steamed Broccolli w/ Dill 184
Bob's Smothered Broccolli....................................185
Summer Italian Vegetables • Baked Onions.................186
Garlic & Her Poor Cousin Onion..................................187
Garlic Butter...189
Basil/Garlic Butter • Herb Butter 190
Sugar & Spice & Other THings Nice...........................191

Snacks & Desserts 193
Fanny Pack Snacks 194
Venison Jerky.. 195
Dutch Oven Nachos 196
Quick Snack & Blackberry Dump Cake 197
Lisa Martiny's Quick Fruit Roll-ups 197
Cindi's Apple Crisp 198
Trish's Rhubarb Crisp 199
River Runnin' Berry and/or Fruit Cobbler 200
Redhot Rhubarb Upside Down Cake 202
Pineapple-Apricot Upside Down Cake 204
Cindi's Pineapple Upside Down Cake 205
Dan Miller's Upside Down Cake 206
McLain's Quick and Easy Cake • Fried Apples 207

Ellis
Pendergraft

ACKNOWLEDGEMENTS

There are many things in life one can do alone. Believe me though, writing and publishing a book are not among them.

The nature of the beast is that I get the "official credit" because my fingers tapped the computer keys and remembered to hit the "Save" key at the appropriate time. But, in reality a major part of the credit must go to the camp cooks who so graciously shared recipes with me.

Special thanks go to Tom Beck, Mike McLain, and Dan Miller of the Colorado Division of Wildlife, who first shared their recipes along banks of various western rivers. Their friendship, plus the recipes, made for dinners truly worth remembering. Also, special thanks go to fellow employees of the Idaho Department of Fish & Game who originally contributed recipes for *Idaho's Wild 100 Cookbook* and allowed them to be reprinted here.

I also wish to thank the Wyoming Game Wardens' Association for permission to reprint *"Game Warden Scramble"* and *"Brother-In-Law Duck"*. Others who deserve special mention include all my ex's; Mike Brogliatti and Bob Jackson— old roommates, and Candis Donicht, my ex-wife, all three being great cooks who were never stingy with recipes or garlic.

One of the perks in my job is getting to visit other folks' camps and often times share a cup of coffee with the cook. On more than one occasion cooks, whose names now escape me, passed on tips, recipes and wisdom, so thanks to those whose names I've forgotten.

Thanks also to the characters in my stories, some named and others, for various reasons, un-named, whose contributions to this book may have been unwitting. Speaking of stories involving others, since they are based solely upon my recollection, I take sole responsibility for any inaccuracies of the events portrayed.

Like any good cook I've saved the best until last. Mike and Cathy Robertson, my publishers, put their faith up front when they approached me about this project. They deserve more thanks than I can put in words.

Cindi Ferro shared her recipes, sliced, diced, cleaned up my messes, and stood over my shoulder while I typed this manuscript, making corrections as I went. Thanks Cindi! Lastly, I must thank my favorite hunting, fishing, rafting, horse packing pardner who also doubles as my son, Brian Welch, aka B.J.

C.W. "Butch" Welch
aka "Cee Dub"
The Old Rock House
Lake Lowell, Idaho, May, 1996

C.W. and a young B.J. Welch in May, Idaho
December, 1986   C.W. Welch Photo Collection

Foreword

Few things in life are written in stone, cookbooks and 'forewords' included. This printing reflects the changes in our lives and in this cookbook since it was first published. Butch a.k.a. Cee Dub and I first met when he worked for the Inter-Agency Grizzly Bear Study in 1975. We reconnected in December of 1996 at a book signing just after this book was first published. One thing led to another and we married in September of 1998. In lieu of a honeymoon, we spent that fall juggling Butch's schedule as a back country game warden around the shooting schedule for his Public Television Series, "Dutch Oven and Camp Cooking." Due to weather and scheduling, we shot only eight shows that fall. I then made my first foray in the publishing field that winter when I revised this book for the second printing to include recipes used on the TV show.

The success of those first eight TV shows surpassed our wildest expectations! Within a few months Butch filed his retirement papers early, and we began traveling around the country 'spreading the word' about Dutch oven cookin'! As our first anniversary passed, we spent September of 1999 preparing for and shooting eighteen new episodes for the public TV series. When winter settled over the South Fork of Clearwater River, we upgraded our computers and software library and took the plunge into the world of publishing. Butch finished writing his second cookbook while I learned the software necessary to transform the manuscript into a finished product. The second cookbook, *More Cee Dub's Dutch Oven and Other Camp Cookin'*, was released on April 1, 2000.

And to what can the success of two cookbooks and a popular TV cooking show be attributed? The answer is easy... Butch! He's unique! As many have said, "He's a natural!" Everyone who knows and meets Cee Dub sees the heartfelt passion he holds for teaching Dutch oven and camp cooking; and sharing his depth for life's experiences both as a "people person" and an avid outdoorsman, which includes laughing at himself. His entertaining delivery, in print or on the screen, is grounded in combining his cooking expertise with his storytelling abilities. No one ever goes away hungry or bored, and he truly has touched many lives!

Cee Dub would tell you that without all the others who have shared their recipes, time, friendship, and the warm campfires, he would not have been able to complete the cookbooks and the TV shows. To all the many friends who've offered their generous support, we both offer our sincerest gratitude and appreciation. We hope that you all enjoy the recipes and stories as much as we've enjoyed bringing them to you. We look forward to long and continued friendships as we embark on our journey. See you in camp!

Penny L. Welch, Publisher
Back Country Press

ABOUT THE AUTHOR
──── by himself ────

An introduction to Cee Dub...

Cee Dub at one of his favorite back country patrol cabins.
November, 1982   C.W. Welch Photo Collection

First of all, I bet you're wondering how someone came up with the moniker of Cee Dub. When I was born, it was quite common for the first son to be named after the father. In my case, I ended up the one and only son and so ended up with his name. Anyway...all I will tell you here is that my initials are C. W. and that from a very early age my Dad called me "Butch."

That pretty well got me through situations as far as family and friends went. But, my real name caused me grief around the play ground at school after a teacher would call me by my real name. By the time I got into college it was my standard procedure to tell my professors to either call me by Butch or by my initials, C. W.

During the 1980's I started doing a lot of white water rafting both in my job and with friends. Over time we gave each other "river handles" similar to truckers, CB radio "handles". One of my river pards, Jim Van Ark, of Challis, Idaho, some how turned **C.W.** into **Cee Dub!** So I hope that explains to your inquiring minds how this cookbook came to be named!

Now we've got that out of the way...let's talk about cookin' with cast iron and Dutch Ovens, recipes, and how to put them all together! It doesn't take a mom very long to figure out which recipes her kids like. My three sisters and I all had our favorites and some of those are still among my favorites.

Over the last twenty-five years since I left home, I will still call Mom, on occasion, and ask her how she did something in the kitchen or if she can recall a certain recipe. (Like me, most are just stored upstairs and not on a recipe card.)

Both of my parents were pretty fair cooks in their own right. Dad had spent some time in the service as a cook before they handed him a Garand rifle and sent him to a place called Guadacanal. Mom learned on an old wood cook stove and knows the hassle of keeping four growing kids happy at the kitchen table.

Anyone who's ever eaten my cookin' knows they'll have to listen to some stories before they get to eat. So...I'll tell the one story every newcomer asks to hear before we go any further. It always comes up. How did you become such a good cook?

To answer that, I have to go back to the early 60's. I was just thirteen when my maternal grandfather died back in Omaha, Nebraska, where Mom is from. While the folks went back to the funeral my paternal grandmother stayed with us kids. As a thirteen year old I was a pretty good judge of food and had some basic culinary skills of my own. I could fry an egg, make oatmeal, and boil a hot dog.

Come Sunday afternoon, that week the folks were gone, I convinced my grandmother I would cook Sunday dinner while she took my sisters to church. (To this day I'd still rather cook than go to church.) As was the custom around our house, Sunday dinner consisted of fried chicken, mashed potatoes and gravy, and a vegetable. I figured it would be a snap since I'd watched both my folks cook this meal many times! Like a lot of people I learn best, or never learn unless it hurts or costs me money! This ended up hurting my ego in the worst way! But, back to dinner.

Any good cook knows one of the real keys to cookin' is getting everything done at the right time. At this I was a failure. The first thing I did was peel and put the spuds on to boil before I started frying the chicken. As was the custom, the chicken went into a brown paper grocery sack with some flour, and salt and pepper before being put in the pan. Up to this point, all was going fairly well.

By the time everyone got home from church, things had started to deteriorate. The corn was scorched, the spuds were soupy from being boiled for double the length of time required, but the chicken would of made Colonel Sanders proud. Fried just right! Now comes the bad part, I'd never made gravy before, but I'd watched mom and dad make it often. All they did (I thought) was dump the flour out of the paper bag, stir it around, and then add some milk. Simple, I said to myself.

I was on the right track, but just didn't get the proportions right. I used approximately the same number of cups of flour when I should have used that number of tablespoons. It took nearly all the milk in the fridge just to thin the gravy enough so that we could mash our potatoes and spread them **over** the gravy! Not a good situation!

The teasing, which later became ridicule, started as soon as Mom and Dad returned. As is the nature of parents, the first questions they asked on their return were "How did things go? Did you have any problems". Quickly and with graphic detail the folks found out about **my** problems!

From that point forward every time we had company, and heaven forbid when in high school and one of my girlfriends came over, every one got a blow by blow account of my fried chicken dinner. I could almost take hearing the story over and over again, but the embellishments and exaggeration wore thin real quick.

Each of us has our breaking point, and I finally reached mine. After being teased for the umpteenth time I finally lost my cool. I lined all three of my sisters up and swore the day would come I would out cook them **all !** Amazing the response a little ridicule is capable of generating. It took some time and a few more failures, but now years later they all agree I'm the best cook in the family. I knew I'd arrived when my two brothers-in-law both confided they preferred my cookin' over that of their wives.

Hunting and fishing with my dad was a big part of growing up. Dad had been raised in the southeast Idaho town of Arimo. I grew up in Chubbuck, Idaho, just north of Pocatello. Our hunting and fishing trips in those days ranged from hunting pheasants right out the back door to deer hunting in the Soda Springs-Georgetown area.

Whether we were fishing beaver dams on Toponce Creek or chasing mule deer in Skinner Canyon, we camped in an old army surplus squad tent and cooked over an open fire or a Coleman stove.

The first time I ever cooked an outdoor meal for myself was in the Boy Scouts. If memory serves me, it turned out worse than my chicken dinner. Burned on the outside and raw on the inside.

In time I got my drivers license and I started hunting and fishing with some of my buddies. For awhile, about all we had for camp fare came out of a can. Somewhere in there, I finally grew up to the point that I thought that steak tasted better than beanie-weenies, and my outdoor cooking skills began to improve. When I left home to attend college out of state, I was able to get by on my own cooking and I'm proud to say now, that I never stooped to a TV dinner.

My first experience cooking for a large group occurred while I was in college. Our Student Chapter of the Wildlife Society held an annual Wild Game Dinner. The dinner itself was being held in a hall seven or eight miles from town. Talk about a logistical nightmare. I had to oversee the cooking of twenty-four entrees ranging from bighorn sheep to porcupine stew. Most of these were being prepared in town and transported to the hall in time for dinner. Besides organizing the whole thing, I then baked fresh baking powder biscuits from scratch for 125 people in one small oven. Looking back now it seems like a blur, but it must have turned out OK because I ended up doing it again the next year.

While going to college I started working as a summer temporary on various research projects for graduate students and for the Idaho Department of Fish & Game (IDFG). Field work meant camping out for extended periods all over southern Idaho. It was during this period that I learned what it was like to control my own destiny. If I wanted to eat good, then I had control by being the cook. Since those early years I've either shared cooking duties, (there are several good cooks in the outfit) or been elected camp cook by acclamation. In 1978 I hired on permanent with IDFG and was assigned to the Challis patrol area.

To digress a minute, during the years between college gradua-tion and being hired permanent, I had several jobs which in different ways contributed to my culinary education. For one summer I worked on a dude ranch in central Idaho, there I was able to observe a couple of pretty fair back country cooks. During the period 1975-1977, I worked six months a year for the Inter-Agency Grizzly Bear Study, (IGBS). We were doing field work in the Yellowstone Ecosystem.

The first two years our field rations consisted of freeze dried food. After all these years, I still consider it a very loose use of the term "food" when applied to freeze dried food. When we would report to work for our ten day shift, we would be met by the secretary with ten days rations in a plastic garbage sack. At this point I began to pay more attention to spices. It became standard equipment to have garlic powder, garlic salt, and various other spices in my back pack.

It seemed that by day two of a ten day hitch, all you and your partner could talk about was what you were going to eat on your days off. We could have written a book about food binging on a couple of occasions. For most of my time with IGBS I was on a trapping team.

During my three seasons, we used a variety of baits, some of which were fit for human consumption. I remember one occasion when the boss told us to go to the store and buy some **rotten** turkey for bait. Just try and go to any store and buy **rotten** turkey. It can't be done! So we got the next best thing——a dozen hindquarter frozen turkey roasts!

Off we went to trap near the Hilgaard Mountains in Montana.

We were staying in an old Forest Service cabin. The snow was so deep that if any bears had come out of their dens, they had headed for lower elevations where snow pack was less. We sat and looked at those turkey roasts for several days while religiously eating our freeze dried meals three times a day. Finally, we couldn't take it any longer. We took the last of our freeze dried rice pilaf and made what looked like dressing and a turkey roast and popped it in the wood stove. To this day, that is probably the best meal I have ever eaten of which freeze dried food was a part.

Anyway...I really began to appreciate good camp food after that experience. Needless to say, when using such things as sardines, honey, slab bacon, cantaloupes etc., enough was diverted from its original purpose to keep the bear trappers in a better frame of mind.

During these formative years I had one other job which would indirectly change how I thought about restaurant food. Between jobs with the IDFG and IGBS, I drove truck cross-country for my uncle out of Omaha.

Someone once said that truck stops must have good food cause that's where all the truckers stop. Wrong! The reason that

Cee Dub and Harold Young are ready to hit the road, May 1985.   Photo by Cathy Young

truckers stop there is because they have big parking lots. Of course this was before "lite" foods came into vogue, and when we as a society didn't pay enough attention to what we were eating. It has changed for the better a little over the years. A steady diet of fried foods eaten at truck stops reinforced my feelings that I could cook better chow than one could find on the road.

Back to being a game warden. The Challis patrol area is now split into two areas with one area having responsibility for patrol of the back country, including a large part of the Frank Church River of No Return Wilderness. It was the eight and a half years I spent there patrolling the back country by horseback, river raft, and foot that I "came of age" as a camp cook. Much of the learning was trial and error, and a whole lot was from spending time in outfitter camps—both big game outfitters and river outfitters. So now, thirty-two years after that fateful fried chicken dinner, I'm writing this cookbook!

Especially if you're a beginning camp cook, hopefully this book will save you at least part of the trials, tribulations, and the ridicule it took me to get this far. So now we're getting close to doin' some cookin'.

ABOUT THE COOKS!

The recipes found in this book represent the efforts and experiences of others and not just the author. A majority of the folks who graciously let me include their camp favorites are (like myself) involved in resource management. As a group, we are not unlike groups of other professionals, in that common bonds are forged not only professionally, but personally as well. Though I can't personally vouch for each individual recipe, I can personally vouch for each of the folks whose recipes you find in my book!

Based on my experience, I think it's safe to say most camp recipes, if researched at all, will result in a story being told either about the cook or the results of his or her cookin'. Most folks have at some time in their life spent at least a little time around a campfire with friends and family.

As our society becomes more urban in nature, I suspect the number of people who've never spent time around a camp-fire will increase. If you stop and think about it, the more our society seems to "progress", the more folks seem to look back in time.

I'm sure social scientists have published numerous journal articles about why "progress" causes some folks to focus substantial efforts into looking in life's "rear view" mirror! Besides the entertainment value, it's the wish of the author for this book to get folks to pause a little after reading some of the stories, to look in their own rear view mirror of life.

Cee Dub, Indian Hot Springs, Bruneau River, April 1994

GOOD COOKS/BAD COOKS!

Cooks come in all shapes, sizes, and with different abilities. Over the years I've been party to some awful good cookin'. On occasion though, I've had meals placed in front of me which would make a TV dinner seem like a miracle from a high falutin' New York City restaurant. Honest mistakes can occur in the kitchen whether it be at home or in camp. Sometimes it is just a brain cramp on the part of the cook, and other times the results fall into that category of natural disasters known as "Acts of God!"

Whatever the reason, the praise when deserved goes to the cook and, likewise, the blame must also be upon his or her shoulders. It would be a dull book which just listed the good cooks I've known over the years. How ever, a couple of cooks on the other end of the spectrum deserve some recognition.

Growing up in the 50's and 60's, several of the national outdoor magazines graced our mail box each month. I remember my dad commenting on an article about some guys on an elk hunt in the Selway River country with an outfitter. Dad said, "if we ever hit the big time, we're gonna go on a hunt like that!" Dad went on to say how much fun he thought it would be to go on a hunt and let someone else do all the camp chores and cookin', leaving a guy with nothing to worry about except hunting.

Raising four kids on a sheet metal worker's wage pretty much precluded that from happening without some unknown rich relative leaving the folks a big pile of money. Reality hit me, just like it did my dad, when I went to work for game warden wages. When I hired on in 1978, I probably could've just afforded one of those hunts advertised in the 50's and 60's!

Anyway.....little did I realize, later events would unfold allowing me to experience two such hunts that had formerly just been dreams of Dad and me. You're probably wondering about now just how relative to camp cookin' this all is. Right? Well, read on!

From June of 1987 until July of 1989 I was the first full time undercover investigator for our department. As an undercover wildlife investigator, we focused, in part, on outfitters. Some were unlicensed, illegal outfitters and others were licensed outfitters who had a tendency to bend things. In cooperation with another western state, I hunted two different big game seasons with an outfitter who liked to bend the boundaries of one of our national parks.

The agency in question felt uncomfortable using one of their officers because of the chance of recognition by the targeted outfitter. As a result I was our agency's contribution and the other state provided the funds and directed the investigation. A dream come true, or so I thought!

Good camp cookin' can be the hallmark of any outfitter whether they a operate a hunting or fishing camp or are just a recreational outfitter. In the two years I hunted with this outfit we endured two different cooks. One washed his hands regularly but was awful short on experience and the other fella knew his way around the kitchen, but didn't wash his hands as often as I think he should have.

I kind of felt sorry for the kid who cooked on my first hunt. This particular outfitter ran an outdoor leadership program for kids during the summer months and some of these kids were later hired on as help during the big game seasons. Most of these kids were disadvantaged and came from big metro areas in the east. (Someone once asked me what I considered back east, anything east of Cheyenne, Wyoming, qualifies!)

As I was saying, as best I could figure out, this was the first job of any kind this kid had ever had. That, plus the cultural shock of a hunting camp, and some over-bearing bosses put this fella at a further disadvantage. More than once, with a cook tent full of anxious guides and hunters waiting for some grub, one of the brothers who owned this outfit would have to tell this poor kid what to do. Not good!

One incident sticks out in my mind. Jerry, my hunting partner from Louisiana, our guide and I got back to camp early one afternoon while every one else was still hunting. Jerry and I walked around camp for awhile to loosen the joints after a day of riding and both ended up in the cook tent. Fried chicken was on the menu. Jerry, being from Louisiana, had more than just passing knowledge of fried chicken as did I, having eaten it every Sunday afternoon while growing up. Just like my first experience cooking fried chicken, this kid did all right on the frying part.

This particular outfit had a big commercial-type propane stove. Most camps wouldn't have anything this big, but our base camp was at the end of the road and they were able to haul this in by vehicle. He cooked the chicken in two big deep pans with about four inch sides. He and the two camp jacks put the chicken in the oven to keep warm, then began to discuss how they were going to make the gravy. About this time Jerry and I looked at each other with raised eyebrows.

We both started to wander so as to get a little closer to the action. In each of the deep fry pans resided about two inches of cooking oil and rendered chicken fat. We both looked on in amazement as the cook put a three pound coffee can of flour in each pan and began to stir it. About this time the two camp jacks allowed as that they thought he needed more flour, so in went another coffee can of flour in each pan. Still it didn't look right to them! While they discussed adding yet more flour, Jerry and I said to hell with bad manners and offered our advice to the cook!

At this point he had six plus pounds of flour in each of his pans which, with the amount of grease involved, would've required a twelve yard cement mixer truck and a tanker truck full of milk to make gravy. From our point of view it would have been fun to watch, but this was our dinner we were looking at. At this point we decided to jump in and help. First, we threw out about ninety percent of what he had started and had no trouble making gravy for sixteen people with what was left. Neither this kid nor I were the first or the last cooks to ever screw up a batch of gravy.

The next year though the cook was different. The kid had obviously cooked in camp before. The first two or three days, the grub really stuck to ones ribs. But, as time wore on I noticed he seldom, if ever, washed his hands.

Elk hunting can be hard work and big appetites result.

Before I go further, let me give you a better mental picture of our camp. The road I mentioned earlier dead ends right on the border of a National Park. It was situated in a large meadow with a crystal clear creek running within just a few feet of camp. We hunters and the guides slept either two or four to a teepee.

Besides the large cook tent, there were two smaller tents for tack and supplies. The horse corrals set on the south edge of camp and a portable toilet set on the north side of the camp exactly eighty seven steps from the door of my teepee!

Anyone who's hunted elk knows how physically demanding it can be. When you are an undercover investigator hunting elk, there is an additional mental challenge.

According to my notes, things started to go hay wire the afternoon of day four. I didn't really feel sick that evening, I just knew that I didn't feel good either. I hit the bed ground just after supper about 9:00 pm. Few things in life hold more terror than waking up in the middle of the night realizing two things. First, you're not sure of where you are at or where the door is. The second is even worse, your belly is telling your brain you have a very short time to locate immediate seating where the place setting consists of a roll of soft paper 4½" in width! This happened to me about 3:00 am after waking from a deep sleep. I didn't count the steps that first trip, that came later. Counting the steps was just something I did to break the monotony of the trip! To say I slept uneasily the next hour and a half would be an understatement.

At breakfast, I felt just so so. Before we left camp I broke into my own private stash of "paper place settings" and stuffed a whole roll into my saddle bags along with my lunch. Diarrhea under the best of circumstances is very unpleasant! Riding a horse and hiking are not recommended activities when one is so afflicted. The side effects induced by a saddle are most unpleasant! Day five of my hunt wasn't D-Day, but it came close to the "Longest Day" in my life up to that point.

I caught some good natured ribbing in the cook tent that night because of my prowess in dismounting a horse, tying it up, and locating suitable cover in record time. Two others in camp mentioned at dinner they weren't feeling all that well themselves. Due to my condition, I ate very sparingly that night. Before dawn the next day I'd made two treks of a hundred seventy-four steps each.

Day six I spent in camp within easy walking distance of the privy. When the other hunters came in that night I had company. One of the owners and one of the hunters were in the same or worse shape than me. In fact, I'd started to feel better and there was more time between treks. Feeling a little better and being very hungry nearly spelled catastrophe. Mexican food is one of my favorites! Despite feeling better, I made three round trips of one hundred and seventy four small steps before dawn. Now another problem began to surface. It came as a great surprise to find a line for the privy about a eighty small steps into my third journey.

Day seven was spent just like day six but with more company. When the hunters came in, it appeared the grub was only sticking to the ribs of half the camp.

Day Eight saw me over the hump, so to speak, and able to get on with the hunt/investigation. To this day, I'm not sure what caused this "adventure", but I do know for sure it made a bunch of people miserable. It might have been clear cold creek water which caused the problems, but since then I've avoided cooks who don't wash their hands very often.

Michael Robertson Photo

Cee Dub keeps the water warm to WASH THOSE HANDS!!!

GOOD HUMORED COOK!

Back in the early 80's, I pulled my pack string into an outfitter's camp just at sunset. Their dudes were still out on the hill, so I accepted the invitation of the cook to stay for dinner. I unpacked and hobbled the stock and packed in an arm full of wood to the cook tent. I poured myself a cup of coffee from the pot on the wood stove and sat down to shoot the bull while the cook started work on dinner. It didn't take long to figure this old kid had spent part of the afternoon visiting with old "John Barley Corn".

The dudes and their guides arrived about an hour after dark. The hot dry weather made the hunting tough, and the elk had all but quit bugling. In four days of daylight to dark hunting the four hunters had hung one small buck and one raghorn bull on the meat pole. Needless to say, there was an air of tired discouragement as we sat around the table waiting for the cook to finish dinner.

The old cook knew how to erase the saddle miles off of one's jeans and the scowl off of one's face. Dinner was roast saddle of venison with red potatoes and carrots, sourdough biscuits, and dessert of huckleberry cobbler! It somehow seemed that after dinner every one's spirits had lifted and that maybe the bulls would tune up and start bugling in the morning.

One of the dudes walked over to where I'd pitched my camp for a little conversation before we turned in for the night. I'll always remember him telling me that no matter how poor the hunting was, just coming back to that tent and having grub that good set before him made the hunt a success.

The next morning I heard the guides wrangling their stock about two hours before daylight. I didn't have to make such an early start, so I fed my horses and wandered over to the cook tent to mooch a cup of coffee. When I pulled the tent flap aside and walked in, the cook was frying ham steaks, and had sourdough pancakes ready to fry, along with a couple dozen eggs. I helped myself to the coffee and sat down at the table. While I sipped my coffee, he cooked. I noticed he was sipping from a glass with about two fingers of an amber liquid. I commented on how good the food had been the night before and that breakfast didn't look like it would disappoint anyone.

As we talked cookin', I asked him where he got all his recipes. When he said he kept them all in his head, I remarked something to the effect that would be kinda hard to do.. "Naw," he said, "they all start with the same ingredient". Puzzled, I asked what he meant. His reply has stuck with me since. He said, "Each recipe starts out with: Pour one beer or one shot of whiskey into the cook! Once I do that, the rest just seems to come to me!"

After eating supper the night before and looking at the breakfast he was preparing, I couldn't see trying to argue with him. This old boy was the epitome of a "Happy cook is a good cook!"

Don't criticize the cook...

It's not written in the scriptures nor is it part of the Ten Commandments, but criticizing the cook or the food borders on the unpardonable. Again I haven't read it in the good book, but sometime, somewhere, a pretty good cook figured out that "Revenge do belongeth to the cook"!

In 1974 after graduating from college, I worked part of a season on a dude ranch north of Challis, Idaho. The first part of the season, we didn't have many guests. The high mountain lakes and trail were still locked in snow so we spent our time shoeing horses, building fence, etc. A fair part of the time it was just the cook and me at the place. She was going to college and this was her first job away from home.

Karen was a right fine cook and knew what she was doing. During the times it was just the two of us at the ranch was about the only time in my life when one person devoted all their energy to cooking for me.

Things went fine for about three weeks. I'd been building fence all day and came back to the cook shack to find a meal fit for a king. Turkey and all the trimmings, right out there in the back woods. After dinner we had pumpkin pie for dessert. My mother was no slouch when it came to pies, and pumpkin was one of her specialties!

After cleaning my plate of the second piece of pie, I shoved my chair away from the table and made what I thought was a very innocent comment. The best I recall now, it went something like this, "that's not the way my mom makes pumpkin pie." I didn't say either recipe was better, nor did I express a preference for one or the other. Just that my mom made her's a different way. Not being overly savvy in the ways of women, I must've missed the dirty looks the cook shot in my direction.

At dawn the next day though, I did notice the quality and quantity of the food had declined. At first I thought it was just the cooks equivalent of a "bad hair day". After the third or fourth day of trying to discern which plate of food was mine and which was intended for the dog, I decided to ask what the hell was going on. The cook had her apron bunched up in her hands and was popping it at flies. After several scowls, which I now saw were directed at me, and after all the flies were killed, she finally spilled it. She thought I didn't like her pumpkin pie!

I finally convinced her of the innocence of my comment. I've since learned that lady cooks magnify any ill feeling towards the complainant when someone else's mother is mentioned. In my case the food improved and I learned not to talk to the cook about my mom.

Years ago I heard a story which went something like this. On a 1880's trail drive out of Texas about half way to Dodge, the cookie quit. The trail boss assigned the cook's duties to be rotated and the first guy to complain about someone else's cooking would finish the trip driving the team hitched to the chuck wagon. Needless to say the cowboys were pretty unhappy.

No matter how bad the food turned out to be, these old cow pokes would bite their tongues and not complain. About the second time through the rotation, one old feller decided he would do something so bad to the food someone would complain and he wouldn't have to cook again. So as the beans were simmering along, he dumped in about five pounds of salt.

That evening as the cowboys rode to camp to eat in shifts, this reluctant cook figured surely someone would belly ache about how salty the beans were. About two bites were about the limit of what a cowboy would eat before throwing the rest away and going back to the herd to eat dust instead. The old boy riding drag came in after being relieved, hungry enough to eat the skillet. The aroma of the beans started his mouth watering. One bite of beans and he exclaimed, "Damn, these beans are salty", remembering in time to add, "but that's just the way I LIKE'M!!! " I never did hear who ended up cooking all the way into Dodge.

———— Chicken ala S*#T ————

About six years ago, just after I'd moved to the Nampa, Idaho, patrol area, the boss asked me to cook dinner after a district meeting. In those days, my signature dish was chicken caccitiore.

At the meeting happened to be one of my fellow officers who would later become my boss. This native son of Idaho, like many, was raised on a diet of "meat and taters". I'm not saying that Norris had led a sheltered life up to this point, but it would be safe to say he hadn't explored many culinary horizons!

As the night wore on and a few malted beverages consumed, Norris began to refer to my chicken caccitiore as "Chicken ala S*#T"! My daddy always taught me not to get mad, but to get even and then get ahead! I bristled up enough that Norris knew he'd got my goat.

As the years went by and Norris was promoted, he ate enough of my cooking that he reached the point of occasionally bragging about it. Now the stage was set to get even and ahead all in one fell swoop!

A couple of years ago, I came back from a fishing trip to

the gulf coast of Texas with two coolers full of jumbo shrimp and fillets from red snapper, red drum, and sea trout. I called the boss and invited him and his wife to a seafood dinner."Sure" he said, "how about next weekend?"

A couple days before the dinner, I went down to a local fast food restaurant and bought a hamburger—as simple a hamburger as can be made by modern technology. I set it on a plate in the cupboard and proceeded to let it dry out a bit. When Norris and his wife Jan arrived, preparations for dinner were well on the way.

After I mixed him about three fingers of corn squeezings with some cola over ice, old Norris really began to brag on my cookin'! About five years had elapsed between the two occasions, and Norris was about to learn that I'll wait quite a while to "get ahead"! In those five years we'd shared quite a few horse patrols, boat trips, and job related camping trips with no complaints about the chow.

If memory serves me correctly, I'd prepared a dozen or so jumbo shrimp with cocktail sauce as an appetizer, fillets of red snapper poached in white wine with a little seasoned butter and lemon juice, new red potatoes boiled in their jackets and dressed with butter and minced parsley, a green salad, and sourdough garlic bread. All was set on the table except for the shrimp and cocktail sauce, and all was set for pay back time!

I walked into the dinning room with the shrimp cocktail and I set one each in front of Jan and my place settings and presented Norris with his entree! You'd have to know Norris to truly appreciate the look on his face. Have you ever witnessed the pained expression people get when they pass gas in a crowded public place or when they've stepped onto a substance in the grass which twelve hours before was perfectly good dog food? The look on his face said it all ! It had taken five years , but now I was **ahead!**

Our dinners almost got cold, we laughed so long! I haven't yet tried it, but I suspect for old "Mr. Meat & Taters", I could cook up some tofu along with a soy bean burger and get no complaints.

27

DUTCH OVEN & CAST IRON COOKERY
Back Country to Backyard

The guy who coined the term "Dutch oven" is no longer with us, so it's impossible to ask him how he came up with the term.

Many stories and theories exist which try to explain it, but my favorite relates to the purchase of Manhattan Island from Native Americans by Dutch traders. As the history books tell us, this parcel of real estate sold the first time for a mere $26 in beads and other trade goods. I think it's a reasonable assumption that one or two three-legged cast iron cooking pots might have been included in the trade.

It's an established fact these three-legged cast iron pots were one of the trader's mainstays. I'm sure these old traders had a name for them, now long forgotten, replaced by a satisfied customer as the "Dutchman's Oven." Now shortened to Dutch oven or simply referred to as a "Dutch."

In your travels stop at any museum with a display on the movement west by Americans—whether a display of the trappers in the 1830-50 era, pioneers on the Oregon Trail, or jitneys loaded down and headed west to escape the Dust Bowl, search out the kitchen display and in every case you'll see a Dutch oven. Dutches were designed and manufactured when most of the people in this country lived in skin tents or log cabins with sod roofs and outdoor cookin' was the norm and not the exception! The old Dutch, which started life with three stubby iron legs, often ended up having its legs amputated in order to be used indoors on a wood burning stove.

Dutch ovens and cast iron cookware in general have changed very little since the settling of this country. As electric and gas stoves replaced wood and coal stoves, modern America began a search for something better to replace cast iron cookin' equipment.

First they used different and usually lighter metals. Then some whiz kid decided the answer to every cooks' dream would be a skillet with electric coils in the bottom. These first two generations of improvements came with a cost. Food tended to stick, which just irritated the cook, but caused dishwashers to get real peeved. Around the corner waited the latest in technology to save us from sticky pots and pans. Yup, as a result of man going to the moon we ended up with all sorts of spin-off technology which yielded the "nonstick" cookware we have today.

Let the TV pitchmen say what they want, I know of not one instance where the "nonstick", "nontoxic", miracle coating doesn't wear off during normal use. By contrast, those Dutch ovens which were traded for Manhattan could still be around today with just normal care. From my perspective, a lot of time and money was spent to improve something which didn't need it.

Anyway... as our nation began to urbanize after WW II it seems our collective national psyche demanded we modernize our camp kitchens as well. Translated—when the "nonstick", "nontoxic", miracle coating wore off a pan in the house, it was relegated to the camp box. In the west, civilization took longer gaining the upper hand. Westerners have a long held tradition of preserving our heritage. This in part saved the old Dutch oven suffering the same fate as corsets.

The 1950's and 60's saw the "American Urban Renaissance" going full bore. By this time about the only place you could find a Dutch was in a sheep camp, an outfitter's wall tent, or an old line shack. Outdoor writer, Ted Trueblood of Idaho often mentioned Dutch oven meals cooked in camp in his articles for ***"Field and Stream."***

The Dutch appeared to be headed down that long inevitable road to obscurity until the United States Congress intervened. Yes, you heard correctly, Congress, though unintentionally, did contribute to the salvation of the venerable old Dutch oven. Who knows, whether intentional or not, it may be the only thing they ever saved. How, you ask, did Congress contribute to the salvation and popularity of the old Dutch oven? In 1968 they passed the *Wild and Scenic Rivers Act.*

When signed into law, river running on western rivers was just coming into its own. Though both commercial and private boaters relied on Dutch ovens for their river kitchens, I credit the commercial boaters for bringing to the forefront our old friend, the Dutch oven.

Early on, river outfitters began to promote "Dutch Oven Cuisine" in their advertising. For folks experiencing real wilderness for the first time, gourmet meals cooked and served in such rustic conditions came as a complete surprise. Through the 1970's and '80's all types of outdoor recreation boomed. The trusty old Dutch saw its opportunity for salvation and jumped on the bandwagon.

Now, over three hundred years after a Dutch trader kicked in a couple of three-legged cast iron cooking pots as booty in a real estate trade, the Dutch oven enjoys wider popularity than ever before. It has made the move from back country to backyard and weekend cookin'.

Though this book touts itself as a "Camp Cookin' Book," suburbanites should find it applicable to backyard or pool side entertaining as well. Dutch oven cookin' offers unlimited alternatives to the same old backyard barbeque fare. So, take that Dutch out of your camp gear and enjoy it even more in the backyard and hey, using the Dutch doesn't have to stop with that – take it inside and use it in your newfangled electric oven. Camp cookin' recipes work great everywhere!

Poolside or back country- goin' Dutch is the way to go!
C.W. Welch Photo

30

CAMP KITCHENS

Look around just about any place or any time and you will see people making certain difficult tasks look easy. Camp cooking falls in that category. Like any job or profession, having the proper equipment, and being well organized, makes the difference in how happy the campers are after supper.

It doesn't matter whether you're car camping, back packing, horse packing or rafting down a river, if you put the right stuff in your kitchen, the cooking part of the camp chores will be much easier. Basically, your camp kitchen should have everything you would use to prepare the same meal at home. Once your menu is planned, then figure out what pots, pans, bowls, and serving utensils you need. Always include extra serving utensils in case the game warden or some other unexpected guest shows up. Once the meal is over, don't forget a couple of wash basins for doing the dishes.

It would be easy to list everything I think one should have in a good camp kitchen, but everyone who reads this would probably add something they just can't do without. If you do much camp cookin', your kitchen will be a reflection of you. To some people who will here remain nameless, that might be a can opener and a Boy Scout camp kit.

One time on a stakeout the other officer I was with didn't even have a can opener. This adventure started about 2:00 am. one spring morning when I came home from a part time job. Another officer needed help on a stakeout and asked me to meet him at the Salmon office by 4:00 a.m. Some surplus adult steelhead had been planted in a spawning stream where they would be very vulnerable to illegal harvest. The logistics were complicated by the fact we had to drive by the houses of some individuals we suspected might try to take the fish. So, I took a shower, changed clothes and headed for Salmon.

Joe, the other officer, told me not to worry about grub, he would take care of it! Now I classify that comment right along with "The check is in the mail"! Anyway, we left the office and headed out a little after 4:00 am. We arrived and found a concealed observation point in a little patch of timber. By the time we arrived, I had been up for almost twenty-four hours.

We shot the bull and drank coffee until noon. There had been no activity at all. I asked Joe what he had for lunch. He got out of the truck and rustled around in his duffle box and came up with two cans of beef stew, some crackers, and a little one burner stove to heat the stew over. I dropped the tail gate and fired up the stove, then asked Joe where he kept his can opener? "Damn" he said, "I knew there was something I forgot"! I (at the time) had a real nice knife on my belt, but I had no intention of using it for a can opener. So then we spent the next twenty minutes searching every nook and cranny looking for a sharp object with which to access our lunch.

We ended up settling for a hatchet! By this time I was tired and cranky but I managed to open both cans without spilling too much. Just an old military P-38 can opener on a key ring would have save a lot of aggravation! The lesson here is simple. Put some time and effort setting up a kitchen which will meet your needs.

Today's catalogs now tout a suitcase contraption which sets up into an adult version of a doll house kitchen. I tend to be more of a traditionalist. For car camping I have a couple of plastic duffle boxes and for horse packing, a kitchen box made to carry my kitchen.

When I choose my pots and pans, I select those which will nest together whenever possible. These same two plastic duffle boxes load onto my rubber raft and provide the kitchen on raft trips. For doing dishes, I use two new metal oil change pans, which I purchased at the local auto parts store. They also nest together which conserves space. I use small plastic containers with snap on lids for table service, spices, etc. My larger utensils usually fit in one of my larger pots or Dutch ovens. My basic car camping/raft kitchen is set up for about 20-25 people. If I end up having to cook for more I just add more Dutch ovens and more table service. If I plan a meal which requires something that isn't in my kitchen, I make sure to add the extras before I leave.

My horse packing kitchen is altogether different. In the early 70's my folks gave me a Kangaroo Kitchen for my birthday. It consists of two metal halves which clamp together. It's outside dimensions are 16 ½" x 14" x 4" thick. Inside is a two burner propane stove, a grill, and aluminum griddle. With everything out, the two halves can be clamped together to make an oven or separated and used as dish pans. By packing the quart size gas bottle elsewhere in the pack box, I have room for utensils, plates, spices, soap, dish towels, hot pads etc. Everything for four people except coffee cups will fit in it. In addition I will take a ten inch aluminum Dutch which nests inside a twelve inch Dutch. My whole kitchen weighs about fifteen pounds. I haven't seen one for sale since the early 80's.

When you're car camping or on a raft trip, the bulk and weight considerations are not as critical as when horse packing. As you plan the meals for a trip think of what prep work can be done ahead of time and what utensils, pot and pans you'll need in camp to prepare the meal. Whatever type or types of camping you do, the kitchen you choose should be tailored to the job. Like many other things in life there is a line between not enough and too much.

Velvet Falls Middle Fork of the Salmon River - June, 1985
C.W. Welch Photo Collection

____BASIC CAMP KITCHEN____

Lots of folks like to make lists. Some of them end up being obsessive compulsive types who think list making is the most fun one can have while still wearing their clothes. My publisher/editor, I've found, likes lists but I've not yet determined if she fits into the obsessive compulsive category. Anyway...at her insistence, I've put together these lists. Just for the sake of list making, we'll figure you're going to be cooking for three companions during elk season. To keep it simple plan to set your camp up at an undeveloped site along a forest road.

Basic Dutch Oven Equipment List

Cee Dub firing up more charcoal - keep extra coals going in an old coffee can.
Michael Robertson Photo

1	12" Dutch
1	10" Dutch
1	pair regular pliers or Dutch oven pliers
1	garbage can lid
20	lbs. charcoal (I prefer ***Kingsford Brand*®**)
1	can charcoal lighter fluid
1	pair of leather gloves
1	small griddle
1	small wire grill
1	empty-perforated coffee can
1	small shovel or entrenching tool

Basic Kitchen
———— Equipment & Utensil List ————

1   large camp coffee pot
5   plates/cups/bowls/place settings (see below)
1   rubber spatula
1   wire whisk
1   wooden spoon
1   metal spatula/pancake turner
1   can opener
1   paring knife
1   kitchen knife w/ blade 6"-8" long
1   slotted spoon
1   large serving spoon/plastic if you're using sour dough
1   small mixing bowl/plastic or glass if you're using sour-dough
1   large mixing/salad bowl
1   package of 1 gallon size zip locks for left overs
1   package of sandwich bags
1   kettle for boiling water
2   serving plates
2   hot pads
2   dishpans
2   dish rags
4   hand towels
1   rubber pot scrubber
1   5-6 gallon water jug per day you plan to be in camp
2   five gallon plastic buckets-1 for wet garbage, 1 for trash

Words of Wisdom

Make sure you have an extra place setting in case the game warden drops by about supper time.

Basic Camp Supply List

1   Roll of toilet paper for each day you plan to be in camp, plus one extra for emergency purpose

1   Magazine per day to be read while using Item # 1

4   Old newspapers to be used for starting fires or substitutes in case you forget Item # 2

1   Shovel to take to the woods when using Items 1 - 3

1   Axe (a single bit doubles for pounding tent stakes)

1   First aid kit

1   Small sewing kit

2   Boxes of stick matches (I put mine in zip lock baggies)

2   Candles

1   Lantern with extra fuel & mantles (Don't forget the funnel)

3   Rolls paper towels

1   Pump container of antibacterial hand soap

1   Bottle of dish soap

1   Small flashlight with extra batteries

1   Roll cling plastic wrap

1   Roll of heavy duty aluminum foil

1   Box of garbage bags

1   Deck of playing cards

1   Copy of appropriate hunting/fishing regulations

2   Plastic tarps (one to cover extra gear with and one to cover your firewood pile with)

•   Game bags to put your elk quarters in, just in case you get lucky
Extra rope/parachute cord/baling twine, then add another 50' just in case you need it

•   These blank spaces are to put in anything you think I forgot.

_____

_____

_____

_____

Basic Chuck Box List

5 lbs.	Coffee
1	Tea bag in case someone doesn't like coffee
1 lb.	Sugar (only important if folks take it in their coffee)
2	Cans of condensed milk (see Item #3 above)
•	Whatever spices & herbs you can't live without
1 each	Salt & Pepper
1	9.5 oz. dispenser of garlic salt
1	5 fl. oz. bottle of Tabasco
10 lbs.	Dry beans
10 lbs.	Onions
25 lbs.	Spuds
20 lbs.	Flour (In an emergency make sure you have a recipe for bannock)
5	Bulbs of garlic
1	Box of tooth picks (we game wardens usually whittle one)
1	**Large Container of Cooks Oil** (See story entitled **"Happy Cook"**, also Cooks Oil can be used to sweeten coffee in case you forget Item #3)
½	Gallon "regular cooking oil"
1	Package of baking soda
1	Small can of baking powder
1	Mouse trap (You can use it to catch mice if you've nothing else to do, but best used for eliciting loud profane statements from your companions when they sneak out of their bunk to snitch the last piece of cobbler)

Words of Wisdom

A small roll of freezer tape comes in handy in camp. Use it to secure or cover the lids of spices and bottled items.

Gettin' Started

I recommend new comers to Dutch oven cooking start at home in case an Act of God destroys their first attempt. In this case fast food restaurants or a frozen TV dinner are available for backup. A failure in camp could mean being ostracized by one's companions, in addition to going hungry. For proof look up surly in a dictionary and there will be a small black and white picture of tired cold and hungry hunters/campers eating cold instant mashed potatoes with only imitation maple syrup to put on them. Not Good! Practice may not necessarily make perfect but call it an insurance policy if you happen to be the designated cook!

Like everything else in life, certain accouterments may help to convince your companions you are infinitely wise and experienced. So, before heading to elk camp or show casing your camp cooking talents for your in-laws on the patio, pick up the following; a pair of heavy leather work gloves, an old pair of kitchen tongs (make sure you get the metal ones), a pair of pliers, and a small shovel. Unless your "Home is on the Range" you should get a firepan. They can be purchased any place which sells river rafting supplies. The deluxe models retail for over $100.00, you might want to consider something less fashionable, but just as good. I use metal garbage can lids. In this day and age of polymers and plastic, metal garbage cans will soon be considered antiques, but they work great if you can find them. I acquired mine by getting up at 3:00 a.m. and cruising city streets on garbage day after a big windstorm the night before. I considered any windblown lid without a name stenciled on it to be homeless!

Planning ahead will help you retain whatever status you have as a cook when you embark on this new endeavor. In the kitchen one merely has to twist a dial to first of all obtain enough BTUs to cook with and thereafter to adjust the heat. Not so with your Dutch! Start your charcoal briquets about 30 minutes before you wish to start cooking. For your first meal try a stew or something similar which requires a cooking time of less than 1 ½ hours. Good charcoal usually provides enough heat to cook that long. If the weather happens to be cool and breezy allow a little more cooking time.

For those of you who like to spend your time counting as you cook, get about 30 briquets started. Slate grey briquets indicate the time has come to christen your new Dutch. For academic puposes we'll make the entree today Great Aunt Mabel's Jack Rabbit Stew (The Basic Venison Stew is a good one since I couldn't get Aunt Mabel's recipe!) Using your shovel, put about half your briquets on the firepan. (I start my briquets on one garbage can lid and transfer them to the one I'm cooking on.) Arrange half the briquets on the firepan so they're evenly distributed where the Dutch will set over them. Using your tongs, place the remaining briquets evenly around the outside edge of the lid with three or four spaced over the center.

While it cooks, you'll have plenty of time to set the table and make sure the floral center pieces are correctly arranged. After an anxious hour's wait, your career as a Dutch Oven Cook will be launched once your in-laws taste this rare delectable treat! For years to come your kin folks will regale others with totally truthful tales of your first culinary triumph using a Dutch Oven!

Throughout the recipes in this book **"DO"** is the abrreviation I use for Dutch Oven.

Camp Cooking with Dutch Ovens

DUTCH OVENS
_____ Selection and Care _____

Like people and horses, Dutches come in all shapes and sizes. For example, at this writing I own twenty-nine different Dutches, including cast iron and cast aluminum, in eleven different sizes.

No matter what you want to cook, whether at home or in camp, you can find a Dutch to fit your needs. A good Dutch oven, properly taken care of, will last a lifetime.

Someone just getting started in Dutch cooking might be confused by the different sizes and trying to decide between cast iron and cast aluminum Dutches. Dutches may be labeled in one of two ways. Some you find list the capacity, i.e. 6 quart. 8 quart. etc., while the more common method is to measure the diameter of the oven. For the sake of consistency, I refer to Dutches by their diameter. In addition, Dutches of the one diameter may also be offered in a "deep" model. These deeper Dutches tend to be about 1" to 1 ½" deeper for the same diameter.

If such a thing as a standard size Dutch exists, one would pull out one 12" in diameter. Most recipes in this book use the 12" Dutch. Why? Because most beginning cooks are going to start with one pot meals which feed about five or six hungry mouths.

__ CAST IRON vs ALUMINUM __

The original Dutch ovens were traditionally cast iron with cast aluminum Dutches having been around for the last 20 to 25 years.

Those of us old enough to have ways to be set in prefer the traditional cast iron Dutches for the most part.* However, aluminum Dutches, because of their lighter weight, occupy a niche in my camp kitchen. My 12" cast iron Dutches weigh between 18 and 19 ½ pounds apiece. A 12" aluminum Dutch on the other hand only weighs around seven pounds, almost two thirds less than the iron Dutch.

Besides being much lighter, the aluminum has a couple other advantages. First, they are easier to care for because they don't have to be "seasoned" or "cured". Because they don't require seasoning, one can use soap and/or abrasive to clean with if the aftermath of dinner turns out to be a world class sticky pot.

The primary drawback to aluminum Dutches I see is this— in cool or cold weather, foods baked in aluminum Dutches do not brown near as well as the same baked goods done in an iron Dutch. The aluminum Dutch, being two thirds lighter, doesn't retain heat long enough for things to brown. The cooler air conducts heat away from the aluminum too fast. For most applications, however, they are fine.

I recommend using aluminum Dutches whenever weight is a concern. For horse packing, I use a 10" aluminum Dutch without legs which nests inside a regular 12" aluminum Dutch. Together they weigh about 11-12 lbs. Plenty of pot capacity for four hunters packed back into an elk camp. When I put a kitchen on my cataraft I also go aluminum. The group I raft with, at times will provide 24 hungry mouths to feed. A ball park figure is one 12" aluminum Dutch per six mouths when planning main dish meals.

* See Table of Dutches for comparative weights of my Dutch collection.

SELECTING and BUYING
———— a DUTCH ————

Before you start to shop, first decide on the size which best fits your needs and choose between iron and aluminum. Making those decisions first should simplify the process. Like shopping for anything else, a few hints on what to look for ensures you're getting what you pay for.

If buying a horse or admiring a pretty woman, I always look at the legs first. The same goes for a Dutch. Check the legs for casting defects to make sure leg length is equal and they aren't bent. The lid should fit easily with a small amount of play if moved side to side on the oven. This play should not exceed ¼ inch. With the lid on the oven the lid should freely twist for a complete revolution without sticking. Inspect the inside of the oven as well. On occasion one will find casting flaws which leave an area of thin metal. I'd avoid buying an oven with this defect. Sometimes in the casting and finishing process a tiny bead of slag will escape the inspectors eye. Normally these can be removed easily with a file and the area smoothed with automotive sand paper.

Some of the best bargains on Dutches and other cast iron cookware are found at yard sales. Use these same criteria, but look for cracks and warping as well. If you find one with the inside all covered with rust look closer before you reject it. Scratch the rust with a fingernail or your pocket knife. Look to see if the bottom is pitted. If it's just rust, you probably just picked up a good Dutch for a song.

_____DUTCH OVEN CARE_____

I can't think of a single item in my camp gear with more potential for longevity than an iron Dutch. No matter what it is, anything will last if properly cared for. Consisting of only two parts it requires just a little care to last a lifetime.

Of the two, aluminum Dutches are the easiest to care for. They don't require seasoning as do iron Dutches. I use hot soapy water and a kitchen scrubber to clean my aluminum Dutches. If the aftermath of dinner turns out to be a cheesy imitation of the LaBrea Tar Pits, just attack with steel wool or any kitchen scrubber. After washing, make sure they are dry and place a paper towel inside before replacing the lid.

Iron Dutches require more care. On a new Dutch just follow the manufacturers directions. Used and or abused Dutches may require a little more work. The worst case of an abused Dutch in my experience occurred on the Middle Fork of Salmon River.

While checking big game camp sites one summer I found a 14" Dutch covered with ashes and dirt in a fire pit last used the preceding November. Both my old black lab "Snoose" and I gagged when I took the lid off. The dinner left over winter in the old Dutch went far beyond a junior high science project. I turned the old Dutch on it's side to allow the contents to ooze out. After collecting old tent poles, jury rigged

43

corral poles and a pile of plastic baling twine, I started a bon fire. Once it got going real good, I set the oven and lid in the fire with a green pole. When I raked enough coals off to the side to broil a steak the old Dutch glowed cherry red. The next morning I took the Dutch and stuffed it up under an old blow-down yellow pine, upside down where it wouldn't collect water. That fall while on patrol through the same area I re-trieved the old Dutch and packed it down to one of my patrol cabins.

I completed rehabilitating the old Dutch the following spring when Terry Williams and I flew in to open the cabin and start the irrigation system. Rust covered the Dutch inside and out when I pulled it from the rafters. After dinner I set both the lid and the Dutch in the coals of our dinner fire. Once it warmed up I poured a small amount of vegetable oil on both and wiped it around with a paper towel. When they began to smoke I pulled both from the fire and allowed them to cool. I repeated the process three or four times a night for a couple of days. By day three we were frying eggs without them sticking. Fourteen years later the eggs still don't stick!

Once an iron Dutch gets well seasoned, cleanup becomes a breeze. If no food residue remains I wipe them out with a damp dish rag and dry with a paper towel. Be sure to treat the lid just as you do the oven as condensation forms on the lid and causes rust. When both are dry, pour about a teaspoon of vegetable oil into the Dutch and wipe both it and the lid with a paper towel to leave a thin film of oil. Don't over do it with the oil because an excess of oil will turn rancid and become varnish like.

Store your Dutches with the lids on in a cool dry place where they won't be exposed to excessive moisture or humidity. Prior to storing for extended periods I always fold a paper towel in thirds and put it in the Dutch to absorb any moisture or condensation which may occur.

DUTCH OVEN
DO'S AND DON'TS & TIPS

Don't use a Dutch to store food in. Once your oven has cooled take care of left overs and clean the Dutch. Acidic foods if left in an iron Dutch will remove the seasoning (cure) of the Dutch and cause food to discolor.

Do allow a Dutch to naturally cool. Cold water poured into a Dutch will cause cracks and/or the Dutch to warp.

Don't put frozen food in a Dutch and then heat it up to facilitate thawing. That's just like pouring cold water in a hot Dutch.

Do heat your Dutch slowly the first few times you use it. i.e. place equal numbers of coals top and bottom five or six at a time.

Once the lid is covered with coals, **do** check to see that the lid spins freely on the Dutch. If it doesn't, once it cools, dress the mating surface of the lid lightly with a flat file. (Aluminum Dutches seem to be prone to sticky lids)

Words of Wisdom _____  _

Use an aluminum foil liner when baking cakes or pies in your Dutch. Make sure that the lid fits tightly and that the foil isn't in the way of a snug fit.

Level your firepan or cooking area before you start cooking. Usually a few shovelfuls will do the trick. To level your Dutch, put 1-2 tablespoons of water in the Dutch, if it rolls to one side or another, level accordingly.

TABLE OF DUTCHES

Cast Iron Dutch Ovens

DIAMETER	WEIGHT	CAPACITY	SERVES
5"	3 ¾ #	1 qt.	1 - 3
8"	9 ¼ #	2 qts.	2 - 6
12"	18+ #	6 qts.	6 - 18
12" Deep	19 ¾ #	8 qts.	6 - 25
14"	24 ½ #	8 qts.	8 - 28
14" Deep	27 #	12 qts.	10 - 34
15" Deep	46 ¾ #	14 qts.	a lot of folks
16"	33 #	12 qts.	12 - 38

Aluminum Dutch Ovens

DIAMETER	WEIGHT	CAPACITY	SERVES
10"	4 ½ #	4 qts.	2 - 8
12"	7 ½ #	6 qts.	6 - 18

Sharon Watson Photo

As you can plainly see, these junior camp cooks struggle with a 16" DO...

DECKING YOUR
DUTCH OVENS

Dinner for 23, Middle Fork Salmon River, 1989
Bob Jackson Photo

Take a tape measure and check the length of the legs on your Dutch oven. Mine all measure from 1 ½+ to about 2" and with the metal trivets I use under my legless 10" aluminum it Dutch also measures about 2". These legs which make it possible to put charcoal or coals underneath a Dutch allow the charcoal on the lid of one Dutch to also cook something in another Dutch placed on top. Depending on the type of dish you're cooking you can often deck (stack) your Dutches to make more efficient use of charcoal and firepan space.

My copy of the Guinness Book of World Records does not list a category for the most Dutch ovens decked up with food cooking in them. However should they ever entertain the notion of such a category, I will submit photographic evidence, plus a list of twenty-two witnesses who will attest to a dinner cooked by the author on the Middle Fork of Salmon River in 1989. In this case, the menu included chicken cacciatore, rice, steamed cauliflower with cheese sauce, and sourdough french bread, all cooking in Dutch ovens decked nine high! Should you wish to attempt such a feat yourself, it would be an understatement on my part if I just said, **"BE CAREFUL"!**

This deck of Dutches contained six aluminum 12" Dutches and three aluminum 10" Dutches. Since my ten inchers were without legs, I used three river rocks to set them on as I completed the deck. The two bottom Dutches contained the cacciatore, with the steamed cauliflower with pepper cheese sauce placed third. The brown and serve circular loaves of bread occupied the other three 12" Dutches. Rice, to serve with the cacciatore, topped the deck of the three 10" Dutches.

I started out by cooking the two Dutches of cacciatore for about 30-40 minutes before I decked them. With about 12-14 briquets on the lid of the second cacciatore Dutch, I set the cauliflower on to steam which took about 15-20 minutes. To warm the bread, I put approximately 12 briquets around the outside of the lid of the cauliflower before I set the first Dutch of bread on. This was repeated for the other two Dutches with bread. Because I just needed to warm the bread, those three Dutches were only in the stack for 10-15 minutes. The rice, in three 10" Dutches which had been started in another firepan were decked atop the bread to finish cooking. Each 10" Dutch had about eight briquets underneath to finish steaming the rice which only took about 10 minutes.

Good planning allowed me to cook this meal with about a third the charcoal it would have required if I'd cooked each dish separately. The question begs to be asked at this point. Do I recommend going to such lengths and 'heights' to save some charcoal? No! But sometime when you're feeding a group something easy like stew you might try it.

THINGS I DON'T CARE TO EAT

One of the advantages of writing your own cookbook is being able to leave out your least favorite foods! In my case it's grits and green lima beans. Two things that I figure you eat just before you eat each other! In college one of my roommates was from Florida. Despite the Southern genes in my system, Tom, my roomate, was unable to convince me grits were real food.

At the risk of offending those who may care for grits, I didn't include any recipes utilizing them. In today's society it is often fashionable to blame one's adult dysfunctions on a troubled youth. Looking at grits, no matter what you put on them, reminds me of the gallons and gallons of hot mush I ate as a kid.

Nothing against my mom, but by the time I left home, I'd more than had a belly full of mush. Tom tried several remedies on grits when we lived together. Eggs with runny yolks, lots of butter, gobs of melted cheese, nothing could disguise the fact that grits look like hot mush. The other Southern dish I ate as a kid, which I didn't and still don't like, is succotash. I'm not sure who thought to call corn mixed with green lima beans succotash, but I care neither for the name or the dish. Why spoil good sweet corn with lima beans?

Anyway...please, don't feel offended by the omission of these two things if they are among your favorite foods. Indeed, please feel free to make them and serve them with anything you find in this book that they will go with. Just don't give me any credit for the meal, whether good or bad.

_____ IS IT DONE YET ?_____

An all too familiar phrase to cooks, especially if there are kids around. In camp where appetites may border on the ravenous, it may be next on the list of most asked questions in the kitchen after, "What's for dinner?" Nearly every recipe I've ever looked at gave specific directions for temperature and length of time to cook.

In the ideal kitchen environment such directions are usually in the ball park. I've not yet rode into a camp equipped with all the latest kitchen technology plugged into a currant bush. For instance, if your favorite cornbread recipe calls for the batter to be baked in a 400 degree oven for twenty-five minutes or until golden brown, that's pretty easy. One simply has to turn on the oven light and look for the "golden brown" or stick one's trusty tooth pick into the center to see if it comes out clean.

In camp though, there are some other variables to consider, baking the same corn bread in a Dutch oven is different. If cooking a roast or stew it doesn't hurt to take the lid off and check on the progress. When baking in a Dutch oven,

The aromas of a camp meal are one guide to dinner time, but check that watch! Mike Robertson Photo

however, you don't want to do that. Each time you remove the lid, heat escapes. As a result, whatever you're baking won't brown. The charcoal and/or wood coals used can't recover the high temperatures quickly enough for browning to occur.

So, how do you know when something is done when you can't look at it? For dutch oven baking I use a simple smell test. If it smells done, it's done; if it smells burnt, it's burnt; and if you can't smell it, it's not done or burned. Besides trusting your nose, pay attention to the time. If following a recipe, plan on the time called for, plus a few minutes longer in most cases.

COOKING "LITE"

As a kid hunting and fishing with my dad and uncles it seemed like camp cooking consisted mostly of fried foods. i.e. fried taters, fried steak, fried fish, etc. Breakfast started the day with the bacon grease being saved to fry the remaining meals. No one really knew or thought such food, which tasted so good, might cause health problems.

I'm not sure when the first "light" or "lite" foods hit the grocery stores, but now you'd be hard pressed to find any one food category which doesn't have a "lite" side. It seems advertising wars are fought between various brands with the victors claiming to be the "lightest" or "litest"! Like a steak cooked for me in a Wyoming truck stop years ago, I find current advertising of light foods to be a little "overdone"!

Cooking "light", whether at home or camp, shouldn't be such a big deal. The two primary culprits in these "light wars" are fat and sodium, with refined sugars and highly processed foods coming in third and fourth. Of the four, I find reducing salt to be the easiest. I either eliminate it altogether or reduce it by half. Most folks find it no problem to salt to their own taste. The processed foods, aka "convenience foods", have their place as emergency rations, but whether in camp or at home, all one has to do to save one's body and pocket book is cook the old fashioned way with fresh ingredients. Sure, it may take more time, but in the long run it's probably worth it, not to mention the satisfaction of cooking a "scratch meal"!

The fat and sugars are just as easily reduced. With one exception, I've eliminated animal fats from all my cooking. My pie crust recipe calls for lard, so as a treat I continue to use it. I tried vegetable fats, but they just weren't flaky enough. I started cooking "lite" by using olive oil almost exclusively. In and of itself, the current research seems to agree, it's as good for you as any fat can be. To further lighten a recipe just reduce the amount of fat. For instance, if a recipe calls for ½ cup salad oil I use ⅓ cup instead. I've yet to see such a reduction turn any recipe into an unpalatable dish.

Refined sugars are no different. Reduce what is called for by ⅓ or ¼ and you'll detect little difference in most cases. When possible in my recipes I'll substitute brown sugar or honey.

As you look through and try the recipes in this cookbook you'll notice very little butter or other saturated fats used.

A little common sense and experimentation will make "lite" cooking easy. So easy in fact, I'm sure you'll never suffer the embarrassment of someone sending their food back to the kitchen because it doesn't have enough fat.

———— Words of Wisdom ————

If possible stay away from glass containers when rafting or horse packing.
Re-bottle such things as vinegar, oil, whiskey, etc. in plastic bottles.

When you pre-package dry ingredients or put liquid ingredients in plastic containers, make sure they're labeled. (Many years ago, on a Boy Scout trip, this detail was over looked. Someone added liquid dish soap to the pancake batter instead of salad oil. I'll leave the results of that faux paux to your imagination!)

PLANNING YOUR MENU

A menu for a group of people isn't too tough if all you're going to do is line up a bunch of cans, open them, and then dump them in a pot. Like wise, hot dogs on a willow stick are easily accomplished without taxing one's creativity. If you're going to be a camp cook worth his salt, it's going to take a little work and planning. Most of us don't figure it out over night, but here are some tips.

Try to use recipes which are easy to multiply. For instance, if there are four people in the party or your family, choose or plan the menu for that number. Then if your cousin all of a sudden asks his in-laws to join the group for your trip, all you have to do is double etc. your recipe to accommodate the extras. Likewise, when I'm cooking a one pot meal in Dutch ovens, I figure about how many people one full Dutch oven will feed. Normally, I figure 6-8 main dish servings per 12" Dutch. It might vary a little with the recipe, the appetites of the group, or the weather. If you don't think the weather is important, read on. I've taken the same 5-6 guys on a raft trip in the summer. If the weather is hot, everyone's appetite seems to decline. On the other hand let it get cold and rainy and the same group of guys will pack away twice the calories per meal.

When planning meals I always plan for seconds. There is nothing worse than a group of guys who are cranky, surly, and still hungry. In addition, I plan on some sort of reserve in case the trip has to extend a day or two. My reserve may just be some rice and beans, but it's a lot better than fried ice and donut holes!

Just who you are cooking for makes a big difference. For instance, little kids and older folks ,as a rule, tend to eat less. On the other hand, a bunch of guys in elk camp are capable of eating everything, including the slowest pack horse.

COOKING FOR VIPs

As just ordinary people, it seems like once or twice in our lives we end up meeting some celebrity or otherwise famous person. Meeting them is one thing, cooking for them is another. The first time it happened to me was in 1978 when I just got started in Dutch oven cookin'.

At the time I lived in a little town in southeast Idaho, called Wayan. It was so small there were only about 50-60 phones on the entire exchange. I was a Wildlife Tech for the Idaho Department of Fish & Game on a research project. I rented a house, actually a large log house which had been built for a big game outfitter just south of the Greys Lake National Wildlife Refuge. A friend of mine, Rod Drewien, was running a project trying to establish another wild population of Whooping Cranes at Greys Lake. The big news that spring, after the snow melt, was that they were going to film an episode of **Wide World of Sports** at the refuge about the whooping crane project. Of great interest to the locals and especially us bachelors was the list of "stars", of which one would be chosen to do the filming. Of the four on the list, Cheryl Teigs was the only one I didn't really know much about. Anyway...the valley was buzzing when I left for a week's vacation and to attend some meetings in Boise. The only thing I remember of the meetings was waking up the last morning, after way too many barley pops, vaguely remembering I'd bought a dog the night before. After the aspirin kicked in, I kicked myself in the tailbone. Before I could go home, I had to go to Salmon and pick up a female black lab puppy. It's another whole story, but fourteen years later, when I buried that old dog, I couldn't think of a better $75 that I ever spent.

There wasn't much on my mind the night I got home except hoping the pup, who I'd named "Snoose", wouldn't keep me up all night. The driveway at my place was about a half mile long. I'd barely got out of the truck when I saw the dust kicking up behind Rod's truck as he came barreling up the drive. After kicking a few clods and looking at the pup,

Rod asked me what I was doing for the weekend. Nothing special, I told him. He commenced to tell me they were going to film the TV show that weekend and they were looking for a place to have a dinner for the cast, crew, and the refuge folks. My place had plenty of room and was a pretty nice setting and would I consider it? Sure, no problem. Then I asked him who the "star" was going to be. He told me Cheryl Tiegs. The name didn't ring a bell until he showed me her picture on the cover of some magazine. I'd seen her plenty of times, but since I never figured we'd ever do dinner together, I hadn't bothered to stick a name to the face.

Dinner wasn't supposed to be too fancy, just Dutch oven fried chicken, Dutch oven spuds, biscuits, and salad. All washed down with cool carbonated beverages! The cooking would be a joint effort among several of us. Even though I wasn't very experienced as a cook, what terrified me most was only having a week to get the house clean! Somehow between work and having a new puppy around the house I managed to get the top layer of dust off, and anything which would embarrass me, stuffed in a closet. Besides just the dinner, one of the guys from the refuge was going to bring his team and buggy over to pick Cheryl up at the pavement and bring her up to the house in style.

Saturday morning found me kicking the horse muffins out of the yard and hauling in picnic tables. With lots of help in the kitchen, the cooking was a breeze. When we took a break just after noon to sip a malted beverage, the excitement of meeting one of the highest paid models in the country finally hit us, especially us bachelors! Any cook who is expecting guests always has that moment of anxiety just before people start showing up. Having had a roommate in college who was a jockey, I knew that some people had to watch their weight with a vengeance. The anxiety attack hit when I figured Cheryl would be like my old roommate. Nothing fried, just broiled or boiled. From that perspective, our dinner might not be such a hit with the guest of honor. Looking at the menu about the only thing a long legged model might find attractive was the "Honeymoon Salad" i.e. just lettuce alone!

If you've ever been to Wayan, you know to buy your groceries before you get there! At the last minute I drove over to the store to see if they had any "LITE" food. Believe me, there is a lot more of it around today than there was in 1978. I managed to come up with a quart of skim milk and a bottle of reduced fat salad dressing, the brand of which I've never seen again! At that point there wasn't much else we could do.

As time drew near for her to get there, Ralph hitched up the team, and Steve, a friend of mine, and I accompanied him on our saddle horses down to the paved road. Snoose hitched a ride on the buggy with Ralph. I'm sure the "Wayan Welcome Wagon" was the least elegant greeting she ever received! The day in the marsh, working with the birds and riding an air boat had been exciting, but when she saw us, her look of surprise was evident. Halfway down the lane Snoose fell out of the buckboard and cried all the way to the house, going as fast as her stubby little legs could get her there. Puppies are magnets. Within a few minutes she was sitting in Cheryl's lap exchanging kisses! Let me tell you, there was more than one of us who wished we were a black lab pup for just a few minutes!

Anyway, as we started to serve, I explained to Cheryl the menu consisted of a "diet plate" and some Dutch oven cookin'. When told what a "Honeymoon Salad" was, all she said was, "I'll pass". Besides eating her share, she drank a couple of cool malted beverages and complimented the cooks, just like everybody else.

Bread in Camp

GETTING BREAD IN CAMP

I can't remember exactly which chapter and verse in the "Good Book" mentions bread as being the staff of life, but even back then camp cooks included bread on the menu. I'm not saying bread is a must at every meal, but I wouldn't advise trying to feed a bunch of hungry campers for a week without it. Two days would be my best guess as to how long it would take before they got kinda surly. Though not mentioned specifically in the "Good Book", I suspect when Moses headed for the mountain to try and sort out all his troubles, no bread in camp was on his list. Should you forget to pack it or run out, as did Moses and his camp, deliverance through prayer would be an option. (However, don't have high expectations of seeing french toast scattered about on the ground and a six point bull hanging on the meat pole the next morning when you peek out of the tent!)

It doesn't matter whether you're car camping, horse packing, or beaching your raft on a cobble bar, bread can "make a meal". Other than car camping, when space is not such a limitation, packing bread gets to be a real pain. For instance, try horse packing enough loaves of bread into camp to keep five or six hungry elk hunters in sandwiches for a week. You'd end up with one pack horse which appears to be fully loaded, but in reality is only carrying fifteen pounds. Then, no matter how carefully you pack, it's always half mashed when you get to camp. Dough ball sandwiches for a whole week might haunt a camp cook for the remainder of his life. Hope exists though, read on to find out how to get to camp and get bread too!

With but one exception, I never pack store bought bread on a horse or raft trip. On raft trips I will take a couple of the round brown and serve loaves of sourdough bread. These fit perfectly in a 12" Dutch and make great garlic bread on spaghetti night. In place of "sliced bread" I pack flour tortillas and/or pita bread. Both pack in a fraction of the space and with the exception of trying to make french toast, make great substitutes for sliced bread.

This sour dough french, brown and serve loaf is mighty impressive and does well in a dutch.   Mike Robertson Photo

A couple of squeeze bottles with mayo and mustard make off road sandwiches a breeze to fix. Squirt a little mayo and mustard on a flour tortilla, roll up a couple of slices of your favorite sandwich meat and or cheese and you're done. Peanut butter and jelly works for the kids. If you want sandwiches to put in your day pack while hiking or hunting, use the pocket pita bread instead. In addition, the "torts" work just as well as "sliced bread" for sopping up gravy etc.

Fresh baked in camp qualifies as the ultimate bread experience in my book. (Which I like to think is a "Good Book", too.) Whether sourdough, from scratch, or a dry prepared mix, your companions will hold you in very high esteem if your menu includes hot fresh bread. The camp cook who graces his table with such fare rarely requires the power of prayer to deliver him from evil; especially any perpetrated by his companions! *

* The individual (s) who speaks badly of any cook that bakes bread, should be remanded to REMEDIAL CAMPING 101 until a member of the clergy certifies that such a sinner(s), through penance and other sanctions, has admitted the error of his or her ways!

BREAD AND HORSE WRECKS

Thomas Creek landing field, Middle Fork Salmon River,
November, 1985   Bill Boylan Photo

One might think these two topics have little in common and under most circumstances such an assumption would be valid. However, on one occasion I observed the first cause the second! Here is how it happened. The last couple of days of August finds the trail heads into the Middle Fork busy, as sheep hunters head in to set up camp and do some last minute scouting before the season opens on September first. In order to kill two birds with one trip, so to speak, I planned to trail in with four head of stock and work sheep hunters for a few days. When finished, I'd leave two head with an outfitter and pick them up later during elk season. With miles to drive and ride, I left home before the grey light of dawn.

When I pulled into the trailhead and unloaded my stock, two fellows, already there, were sorting gear and making up horse packs. They had two saddle horses and two pack horses in various stages of undress. As I unloaded gear, they hustled over for a little conversation. It took just a few minutes to learn they were headed for Waterfall Creek. They told me they hoped to make it to Pole Creek that night and on into Waterfall Creek the next.

I'll never be a unanimous choice for the "Packers Hall of Fame", but it didn't take an old hand to see these two guys

60

qualified for "Pilgrim" status. (Volume Two of this series will deal with "Pilgrims" in greater detail.) Anyway, they were still within sight of their truck when the first of several wrecks occurred. I watched them try to balance and jury rig the two outsize loads so they'd ride. In order to give them a head start I made up my packs and ate a lunch of sardines and crackers before I packed up and headed out.

Going down the old two-rut road, I saw signs things might be unravelling for these guys. In two different places the tracks showed they'd stopped and re-set their packs. I don't like to bet on someone elses misfortune, but this for sure didn't look like a good bet!

For anyone who's ridden the Camas Creek Trail, they already know Big Dry Gulch offers the only real good spot to horse camp in the fourteen miles from the trailhead to the mouth of Camas Creek. I caught up to these guys about a half mile short of Big Dry Gulch. Where I caught up to them, the trail was not wide enough to get my string past, so I pulled up and waited. Trying to repack kitchen boxes in the middle of a trail on a buzzed up pack horse will try the patience of any saint. Suffice it to say none of the adjectives or adverbs from the conversation between those two belong in a cook book.

I watched as one fellow rearranged canned goods while the other tried to tie a flatland version of a diamond hitch. Among the canned goods, I could see several "cardboard tubes" of store bought, taste like homemade, ready to bake biscuits. These guys knew they were holding me up and were hurrying as best they could. Within about fifteen minutes they were ready to head out again.

As they took off I held back a little ways just for a cushion in case they had more problems. Even from a distance I could hear the canned goods rattling in the bottom of their pack boxes. They'd packed their kitchen on a bay horse who, it appeared to me, had little experience as a pack horse. He kept trying to walk wide of the trail and get up next to his buddy. Within about 200-300 yards of Big Dry Gulch this old bay horse again went wide of the trail, it having slipped his mind, with his load, that he was now a couple feet wider than normal. When the off-side pack box smacked a big granite boulder several things all started to happen at once.

He'd hit so hard he stepped sideways into the horse he was trying to pass. This horse, being ridden by the owner of the offending pack horse, responded by jumping ahead into the rear of the pack horse in front. The chain reaction continued to include the lead horse as well. Now, both riders began screaming various adjectives, adverbs, and non-complimentary nouns!

Up to this point, things weren't too bad. Within seconds, control appeared to be within their grasp. Then the second stage ignited. The horse, who started it all, had just about calmed down when those biscuit-bearing cardboard tubes spontaneously began to explode. I'm not sure what it sounded like to this old horse, but whatever it was, he decided it wasn't in his contract to haul. Every time another tube gave up a load of ready to bake biscuits, this old horse would buck a different direction. For the minute or so it took him to buck the whole load off, he looked like he belonged in a rough stock string on the rodeo circuit! Not to be outdone, the other pack horse got in the spirit of things and both loads ended up scattered over a fairly wide area. For the first five minutes after the dust cleared, the only word I heard either guy say which could be printed here is**"you"**!

Fortunately, no visible injuries were suffered, but I suspect if those two guys ever get ahold of this cook book they'll suffer flashbacks or latent mental trauma for awhile. Anyway... I pulled off at Big Dry Gulch, tied my stock up and gave them a hand. The pack box, which formerly contained the pressurized biscuit bearing cardboard tubes, now held an amorphous blob-like mixture of raw biscuit dough, eggs and egg shells, orange juice, maple syrup, and soy sauce covered cans. We dumped this mess as far off the trail as we could. If only the next party down the trail had been a film crew shooting special effects footage for a sci-fi horror film. In this case a picture would have indeed told a story worth a thousand words. It honestly looked like a quivering, glistening, gob of mutant protoplasm from an alien planet.

An in-depth analysis of this situation might well yield several "morals to this story". i.e. Don't pack pressurized containers on a green broke pack horse; if you do pack such containers, make sure to pad them so they won't release their contents prematurely, or if you want fresh bread in camp, pack the ingredients and bake it once you get there!

A PINCH OF THIS AND
A DASH OF THAT

Sums up my method for measuring recipe
ingredients! I confess I have no idea where
either of my two measuring spoon sets
are as I write this. They might be
stuffed in the back of a kitchen
drawer or then again, they might
be downstairs where I keep stuff used in my catering business
or then again, they might be/could be in a grub box out in
the garage. Really, I don't know!

Most cooks I know fit into one of two categories when it
comes to measuring; some approach anal retentive behavior
when they measure something like baking powder for biscuits. As an example, my recipe for baking powder biscuits
calls for a tablespoon of baking powder. Translated it means a
heaping big spoonful of baking powder, if I grab a regular
spoon from the silverware drawer, or just a well rounded
soup spoon full if that's what is closest. Yet, I've watched
other cooks measure and level precisely one tablespoon of
baking powder to the microgram. Such precise measurement
may be required when measuring plutonium for a small
tactical nuclear war head, but not necessary for baking
powder biscuits.

Yes, when I'm reloading rifle shells I measure precisely, but I
just plan to eat my biscuits not shoot them. Nowhere in
recorded history exists an instance of a biscuit blowing up in
one's face because the recommended load of baking powder
was exceeded. And when both batches of biscuits are tested,
I've yet to be able to discern any difference in the finished
product. Far be it from me to discount the pleasure some
folks get by scraping and peering at their measuring spoons!

Though "close enough for government work" pre-dates my
employment with the State of Idaho, that old cliche fits me
pretty well when I'm in the kitchen or camp. The hardest part

of writing a recipe down comes when I have to put in black and white just how much of what goes into a specific dish. Maybe I should preface each recipe with "all measurements are approximate"! I'll admit someone who carefully measures their ingredients into a measuring spoon rarely ends up dumping the entire container of pepper into the stew, but on the other hand, risks exist in the kitchen, too!

Cee Dub prepares his baking powder biscuits, which have been said to be the best since Great Aunt Maude's.

Mike Robertson Photo

SOURDOUGH

Talk to a "Sourdough Cook" and almost immediately he'll launch into a history of his starter. (You may be reminded of folks who've just become grandparents for the first time!) It's not uncommon for a particular starter to be handed from generation to generation and considered to be a family heirloom. Fanatics, who inhabit the ranks of "Sourdough Cooks", will always like to tell how their starter was carried over Chilkoot Pass during the Klondike gold rush. They say this as if any starter with a less glorious past is inferior. Over time I've found it's easier to let such folks think their inferior thoughts rather than argue with them.

The starter I have used for the last twenty years was given to me by an uncle who lived in the Seattle area. As I recall, a cook off a merchant ship gave it to him only after an hour long discourse on the lineage of this starter. Translated, it means if you buy or are given a starter, it is at least a day old. Don't worry though, "Sourdough Cooks" often like to fish as well and thus, share a trait for which all fishermen are famous. So, within a month or so of starting to cook with sourdough it's perfectly acceptable to me if you want to "stretch the dough" so to speak!

At home I keep at least two containers with starter in them at all times. When I pack for a trip I take one starter with me and leave the other at home. Then should I roll a pack horse off the trail or flip my raft, I'll only be out of sourdough until I get home. The starter I leave at home, I like to think of as my insurance "dough"!

Rather than this author attempting to write another "Sourdough Cook Book", Jack Trueblood graciously allowed the use of his recipes and an explanation of just what "Sourdough" really is. As a kid growing up in the 50's-60's in southeast Idaho, I often read stories in **Field and Stream** written by Jack's father, Ted Trueblood. Ted often mentioned sourdough biscuits and bread when describing camp life in those stories. At any gathering of the Trueblood clan, "Uncle Jack" will be found with his "sourdough fixins", passing on this knowledge to all his nieces and nephews.

UNCLE JACK'S
SOURDOUGH RECIPES

Alaskan "sourdoughs" got their nickname because they used sourdough—a bread dough that would work on the simplest of ingredients and make a variety of products.

There was also a general belief that baking powder, required in other breadstuffs, was the opposite of an aphrodisiac, which made the natural ingredients in sourdough pretty attractive.

To make your own starter, mix two cups flour, two tablespoons sugar, one tablespoon salt and one tablespoon of vinegar in enough warm water to make a creamy batter. Leave it in a warm place for four days to a week until it begins to sour, or "work." If it is ready, it should have bubbles on top. Pour some in a dish and mix a dash of soda with it; if it is active and ready to use, it will respond like hotcake batter (see recipe).

Sourdough "works" because of a culture similar to yogurt. It forms an acid which will attack most metal containers and could poison you, so keep your starter in glass, crockery, or plastic. Stainless steel is OK for mixing batter, but it's not best to leave it in that, or even in a fruit jar with a regular ring and lid. It is imperative to never use any metal pot or metal spoon with sourdough EXCEPT stainless steel, as it causes a chemical reaction. A wooden or plastic spoon is a good idea to go with the sourdough pot. Gas bubbles (carbon dioxide) are released as the starter "works," so don't close the lid too tight!

Sourdough rises because of the gas bubbles, same as bread dough with yeast. The baking soda you add to the batter causes a rapid reaction with the acid in the starter to make the light hotcakes, and also, neutralizes the acid taste. There is no reason for sourdough to taste sour. A slight soda taste is OK, but if you get too much, it makes the bread look yellowish.

When you plan to use your starter, take it out of the refrigerator the previous evening and mix flour and water with it to batter consistency. Let it set out overnight to work. Then you take out as much as you will need for the day, but be sure there is a cup or more left, and put it back into the refrigerator. If you forget it and it molds on top, simply get two or three tablespoons of clean batter from the bottom of the crock and mix with new flour and water.

Never add anything to the starter but flour and water. No yeast, no leftover batter, no potato water or any of the other stuff you hear about. A slightly lumpy starter will work itself out overnight, so it's better to leave it that way than way too thin.

SOURDOUGH HOTCAKE
_____ BATTER RECIPE _____

Ingredients:

2 cups starter
1 Tbsp. sugar
1 tsp. salt
1 egg

Mix well by hand. If you want berries or other goodies, add at the last.

Add 1 tsp. baking soda *[slightly more suits me]* mixed in a dab of water to prevent lumps; stir only as much as necessary to mix; batter should rise to about double, looks kind of like meringue.

Spoon onto hot griddle, turn when bubbles pop, test for done by pressing corner of spatula into center of hotcake. If it springs back, it is done.

SOURDOUGH BREAD

Use same batter as for hotcakes, or use the leftover. Mix in flour until it is too stiff to stir, then knead in more until just barely tacky. Form into loaves and grease (PAM® makes this very easy).

Place in greased pans, cover with a towel, and leave in a warm place to rise. At room temperature, this will take more than 4 hours. If the loaves fill the pans ⅔ full, it will rise until the tops are a bit higher than the pan. *I've never had a bad reaction from using metal bread pans. You can leave it all day if you want* .

Bake 45 minutes to 1 hour at about 350 degrees, or until crust is brown and loaves pull away from sides of pan. Remove, rub with butter or shortening, wrap in towel to cool for a few minutes or serve hot. Placing the bread in plastic bags before it is entirely cool will retain some moisture in crust.

Biscuits are just tiny loaves of bread; adjust the time in oven.

Donuts can be made without rising time. Make a bread dough, roll out ½ inch thick and fry.

Tarts are filled donut dough.

Scones are scraps of donut dough twisted or folded with sugar and baked or deep fried.

Jack Trueblood, Information Specialist
Information and Education
Idaho Department of Fish and Game • Boise, ID

CEE DUB'S
—————SOURDOUGH BISCUITS—————

Ingredients:

2 cups starter
2 cups butter milk
4 - 5 cups flour (don't
   use self rising)
2 Tbsp. honey or sugar
1 Tbsp. baking powder
1 tsp. baking soda
1 tsp. salt

A heap of sourdough biscuits is a sure crowd pleaser!   C.W. Welch Photo

First thing in the morning, after you get the breakfast dishes done; mix the starter, butter milk, and about two cups of the flour in a large glass or plastic bowl. Stir to mix fairly well then cover with a clean dish towel and set in a warm place. Once you get dinner started, mix the remaining dry ingredients and then add them to your starter/butter milk mixture. Work into a smooth dough and knead for about 10 minutes. Roll out about ¾" thick and cut with a biscuit cutter. Place biscuits close together in a Dutch after you butter the bottom. Let raise for 30-40 minutes in a warm place. Put the Dutch in the fire pan with 3-5 briquets underneath and 20-24 on top. Bake for 25-30 minutes.

Two or three times, pick the Dutch up and give it a partial turn over the briquets to make sure the bottoms brown evenly. This recipe will fill about three 12" DO's depending on how thick you roll your dough out.

To make herb biscuits mix ½ tsp. each of celery seed, ground thyme, and rubbed sage with remaining flour and dry ingredients.

POOR MAN'S
SOURDOUGH PANCAKES

More often than not, folks end up with a prepared pancake mix in camp instead of sourdough. Not one to put the store bought mixes down, cause over time I've ate my share, but they're not really in the same league. To put a different spin on the store bought kind try the following. Try replacing the water called for in the mix directions with an equal amount of beer. In camp cook circles a debate exists whether to use stale beer or fresh beer for what some call beer pancakes and what I call "poor man sourdough pancakes". I suppose either would work, but the folks I camp with are not in the habit of opening a beer and letting it set overnight.

A word of caution though! Unless you know the religious affiliations of all who you're cooking for, it's best to tell folks about the beer part of their pancakes **before** they start eating. Telling someone whose religious beliefs don't include making pancakes with beer, half way through a short stack, will for sure cause problems. I found this out the hard way one time.

I had no idea this woman, who shall remain anonymous, came from a prominent pioneer family in a state which borders Idaho on the south. Someone else in camp had just exclaimed something to the effect "it's hard to beat good beer pancakes" when this gal began choking. My first thought was she'd got something "down the wrong pipe" as my Dad used to say. In reality though, upon hearing this comment in mid-swallow, she'd instantly lost her appetite. Visions of having to perform the Heimlich Maneuver vanished when she bolted from the tent, followed by the obvious sounds of an airway being re-established. Since then, I've made sure to inform my guests of recipe ingredients prior to serving.

CEE DUB'S BASIC BISCUITS
plus VARIATIONS

Biscuits for any meal is a treat!
Mike Robertson Photo

Ingredients:

2 cups all purpose flour
1 Tbsp. baking powder
1/8 tsp. salt (optional)
1/3 cups vegetable oil
2/3 cups milk or buttermilk*

Mix dry ingredients. Add liquid ingredients. Stir in bowl. Work with hands in bowl just long enough to form a ball. Pat out on floured board ¾ inch thick. (Do not knead.) Cut and bake in 425 degree oven approximately 20 minutes until brown.

*I've had better luck with a moister dough, using slightly in excess of 2/3 cup.

Herb Biscuits--Add:
1/8 tsp. celery seed
1/8 tsp. sage
1/8 tsp. thyme

Plain Dumplings--Increase milk to 1 cup

Chicken Dumplings--Add ½ tsp. poultry seasoning to flour.

Beef or Venison Dumplings-- Add 1 heaping Tbsp. prepared horseradish to liquids.

Basic recipe serves 4 to 6, depending on size. This recipe doubles or triples easily. A double batch fits just right in a 16-inch Dutch oven. When baking in an oven, use an 8-inch cast iron skillet or cookie sheet, lightly greased.

ANGEL BISCUITS
"BIGMAMA'S BEST"

Ingredients:

5 cups flour (Plain)
1 tsp. soda
1 tsp. salt
3 tsp. baking powder
2/3 cup shortening
Dissolve 1 package yeast in warm water
with 3 Tbsp. of sugar (called "proofing the yeast", it
gets a bit foamy)
2 cups buttermilk

Mix dry ingredients well; add shortening, yeast and sugar mixture and buttermilk. Work up on a floured surface. Don't over work. Put in covered container in the refrigerator. Use as needed. Pat out on a floured surface. I use Crisco to grease the bottom of the Dutch and a little pat of it on the top of each biscuit. You don't have to let these rise first. Cook at 375°. Use 3-5 briquets underneath and 20-24 on top.

These keep well in the cooler or the refrigerator; legend has it up to six weeks. I honestly don't know that, because they never last longer than two or three days. At home I bake these on a round cast iron griddle in the oven until golden brown. Preheat the Dutch or your home oven for best results.

Sara Brown
Twin Falls, Idaho

Words of Wisdom

To make your own pre-packaged stuff, measure and mix all dry ingredients at home and put them in a labeled zip-lock bag.

__DUTCH OVEN CORNBREAD I __

Ingredients:

1 cup flour
1 cup yellow corn meal
1 Tbsp. baking powder
½ tsp. salt
1 egg
1 cup butter milk (or milk)
⅓ cup olive or vegetable oil

Mix the wet and dry ingredients separately then pour wet ingredients into the dry ones. Stir until well mixed then pour into a well greased 10" Dutch. Bake for 20 -25 minutes with three briquets underneath and 14 - 16 on top. Make sure you lift and turn the Dutch a partial turn every 8 - 10 minutes so the bottom browns evenly. Serves 4 - 6

__ DUTCH OVEN CORNBREAD II __

Ingredients:

1 cup yellow corn meal
1 cup flour
2 eggs
1 cup milk or buttermilk
1 Tbsp. honey/or molasses
½ tsp. salt
1 Tbsp. baking powder
½ tsp. baking soda

When making corn bread, I like to grease my Dutch and let it set in the firepan with 6 - 8 briquets underneath while I mix my batter. Sift or mix all your dry ingredients and then add the eggs and buttermilk. Pour the batter into a 12" Dutch and bake for 25 - 30 minutes. Serves 6 - 8

MEXICAN CORN BREAD

Ingredients:

1 cup yellow corn meal
1 can cream corn
1 can (7 oz.) green chilies drained and diced
½ cup grated cheddar cheese
2 eggs
½ cup olive oil
¾ cup milk
pinch of salt
½ tsp. of cumin

In a mixing bowl make a batter with the flour, oil, milk,eggs salt, and the creamed corn. Add cumin or Mexican seasoning to batter and stir until well mixed. Pour half the batter into a 10" Dutch which you've greased. Take the chopped chilies and make a thin layer over on top of the batter. Cover the chilies with the grated cheese and pour the remaining batter over it. Bake with three briquets underneath and 12 - 16 on the lid for 25 - 30 minutes.

Serves 4 - 6

Words of Wisdom

If you're car camping in a developed camp ground, some sort of fire pit is usually provided. When on a trip away from roads end, take a few minutes to select a good kitchen site. A "level" spot, chosen by the cook for his kitchen, takes precedence over someone who wants to pitch their sleeping tent in a certain place. I find it much easier to sleep on a bit of a slant, than cook on a "sidehill". If using a fire pan at home or on a raft trip, suitable flat rocks can be used to level the firepan. If horse packing and cooking with coals from the camp fire, I level the area where I set my Dutches with a shovel. A level Dutch is always important, but especially when baking!

— SARA'S MEXICAN CORNBREAD —
Jalapeno Cornbread with Hamburger

Ingredients:

Batter:
1½ cups corn meal
1 #2 can creamed corn
2 eggs, beaten
1 ½ cups buttermilk
½ tsp. baking soda
¾ tsp. salt
½ cup bacon drippings

Filling:

1 lb. hamburger meat
1 onion, chopped fine
1 lb. American Cheese, grated
3 jalapeno peppers* - seeded & chopped
1 jar (2 oz.) chopped pimiento
2 Tbsb. corn meal

Saute' hamburger meat and remove fat. In separate bowls, have onion, cheese, jalapeno and pimiento mixed. Grease 12" DO . Sprinkle 2 Tbsp. of corn meal in greased DO and brown. Pour ½ of the batter in the DO and then layer jalapeno, cheese, meat, onion and pimiento. Pour remaining batter on top. Bake with four - six briquets underneath and 12-16 on the lid for 45 minutes.

*Mild chopped green chilies may be substituted for jalapenos.

Serve with side dish of pinto beans.

Sara Brown, Twin Falls, ID

CAMP BREAD

Ingredients:

2 cups white all-purpose flour
2 plus tsp. baking poweder
½ to 1 tsp. salt
1 Tbsp. shortening
1 ½ cups evaporated milk
Shortening for frying

Add dry ingredients in order and stir. Cut shortening in, add evaporated milk and mix. Knead slightly, then pull off pieces of dough about the size of a large walnut and shape the dough tortilla fashion into about ¼" thickness. Use fingers to punch hole in center of dough. In your dutch melt shortening until very hot and to a depth which will cover the dough when cooking. Watch closely and turn over once when golden on bottom (approximately 1 minute each side). Remove and drain on paper towels. Serve hot with honey and butter or shake in paper bag with cinnamon and sugar.

Joyce Cowan
Hamilton, Montana

Words of Wisdom

Keep a clean camp! As soon as you set up camp, get a garbage sack set up. Completely burn any dry garbage you can. Food scraps, wet paper towels, non-burnable garbage should be double bagged and put up every night. On a raft trip, the first cooler I empty becomes the trash storage container. On horse back trips, I normally pack it in the box with my hobbles, vet kit, and horse supplies.

CAMP FRENCH TOAST

This French Toast recipe was one that I created at home and perfected on family camping trips. On a whitewater float trip I innocently volunteered to help good friends, Bob and Donanna McKinstry, fix breakfast. I mentioned that French Toast would be quick, easy and should satisfy the boating crew's first morning's hunger. No trip since has gone by without French Toast and is a staple at Camp Robertson.
Mike RobertsonTwin Falls, ID

Ingredients:

1 to 2 dozen eggs, depending on number of hungry folks
1 to 2 loaves french or sourdough bread
Milk
White wine
Tabasco® sauce
Salt, Pepper, Mrs. Dash®
1 or 2 cubes butter melted to semi-liquid

Break first dozen eggs into mixing bowl, add in about ½ cup milk, ¼ cup white wine and three or four "dollops" of tobasco sauce. Sprinkle surface of mixture with salt, pepper and Mrs. Dash®. All that seasoning may look like too much, but it isn't. Whisk vigorously with a metal whisk, add semi-liquid butter and whisk until mixture is well mixed. Pour into a long, wide flat cooking pan or dish. Place as many slices of bread as the pan will hold, letting the bread soak up the mixture. Turn bread over in mixture until second side has soaked up mixture.

Cook on preheated griddle. I prefer seasoned cast iron or rolled steel. Flip after first side is golden brown. When second side is done, serve with warm syrup, berries, honey or jam.

Repeat above mixture for second go around.

Note: Since the cook seems to always eat last, use remaining mixture for great scrambled eggs for yourself.

Meat in Camp

BARBEQUE
TEXAS STYLE

When you're born, raised, and educated in SE Idaho the mention of a particular dish conjures up certain memories. For example, spaghetti brings visions of Italy, chow mein makes one think of China and the mention of BBQ brings to mind the Lone Star State.

In the universe of BBQ, Texas is real close to the center, while SE Idaho is on the very fringe, kind of like the planet Pluto. Where I grew up, good BBQ consisted of a thick brownish ketchup-like substance one occasionally found at the grocery store. When you don't know any different, you tend to think this is as good as it gets!

My introduction to real Texas BBQ didn't occur until the late 1970's. While trapping grizzly bears for the U.S. Park Service in and around Yellowstone National Park in the mid 70's, I met a group of Texans. I'd been sent into their camp to trap a marauding bear. I didn't catch the bear, though I did catch the outfitters' Black Lab, who was known as Bumper. From the point of view of my boss, I didn't accomplish a lot during those ten days. That's his point of view. From mine it was different. The friends I made there, on Fishhawk Creek in Wyoming, are still friends to this day. Though it didn't happen for several more years, it was while visiting them in Texas I finally learned what real BBQ tasted like!

Now, if you've got this far and you think I'm about to reveal the secret of real Texas BBQ, you are dead wrong! This story is about a Texan who attempted to apply the principles of BBQ to one of Maude Garroute's goats.

By the early 1980's I'd been hired as a game warden and was stationed in the little central Idaho town of Challis in Custer County. Some of you who read this will have been to Challis and/or lived there, so this next part you can skip over. This will really ring true to any person (especially if you're single) who works for a natural resource management agency and has been assigned to a central Idaho cow town. More succinctly put, look up "social isolation" in the dictionary and you'll find a picture of some single folks (all agency types) doing a backyard cookout in the only county in this state named after a loser!

Bear with me, we'll get back to Texas BBQ, but first let's take a closer look at the picture in the dictionary. Henry Ketchie, the only one of the group who'd gotten married before being sent to Challis died a few years later from cancer. One fellow ended up being a famous author and photographer. One of them is writing his second cookbook. Several of them were never seen after that summer, and one of them hailed from the land of BBQ.

McKinney's folks ran cows on a little place outside of Atlanta, Texas, which is not too far from the Louisiana line. After finishing college, McKinney, like a lot of us, needed to see the "wild west" and headed out. He ended up working for the Forest Service on a summer timber marking crew. His boss, my good friend, Henry Ketchie and I started spending a lot of our time together. Like other transplants as the leaves began to turn color, McKinney's thoughts turned to hunting.

Enter Maude Garroute and her goats. If you know anything about the geography of central Idaho, you know Challis has always been one of the primary access points to the Middle Fork of Salmon River. Maude had lived in the Middle Fork in the early part of this century. Maude, like other "hard scrabblers" left the back country and spent her last years near town.

As the local game warden, I tried to keep up on the local wildlife. Not long after moving there in 1978, I saw a bunch of what appeared to be feral goats hanging in the rocks near the mouth of Morgan Creek. When asked, an old timer told me they'd belonged to Maude Garroute. Even back then, what knowledge I gained about Maude was probably 50\50 fact vs. legend. Suffice to say both local legend and old timers said Maude fit into the "eccentric" category. Maude had passed on some years before I got there, but her little band of mixed breed goats still hung around in the ledges and cliffs just north of the mouth of Morgan Creek.

Archery season opened around September first as I recall. McKinney forked over the big bucks and bought a nonresident license, along with a deer tag and an elk tag and headed to the hills with the hordes. The success rate for archery hunters is fairly low. I've seen these low success rates translate into disgruntlement! My pard from Texas was no exception. He was getting the same attitude as one expressed by one Buzzard to another in a poster from back in college days; "Patience my ass, I want to kill something."

One day I looked down the lane and saw McKinney's old brown Ford pickup truck leading a cloud of dust towards my house. After offering me a cold barley pop, McKinney started telling a story which I could tell was leading up to something. (About now, does that sound familiar?)

Being the local arbiter/authority on what seasons were open and/or closed, McKinney inquired as to the status of Maude Garroute's goats. "Would it be legal to archery hunt them?" he asked!

Halfway through the six pack of cold barley pops, and thumbing through the Idaho Code book, we decided there was nothing written to prohibit the taking of feral goats with archery equipment. McKinney didn't hang around long after that, nor to my knowledge did he seek a second opinion.

It was getting to be my busy time of year, so if folks wanted to get a hold of me they usually had to work at it for awhile. (This was pre-answering machine era) Anyway....one evening about a week later, I saw the same brown Ford truck leading a charge of dust up my road just as I was getting ready to go to work. No preamble from Mckinney this time. "Would it be legal to shoot one of those goats with a center fire rifle?" There had been no mention of feral goats in the archery regulations and a search of the general big game regulations yielded the same. There was just something about the way Mckinney was in a helluva hurry to get the answer he wanted and get back down the road. Being a nosy and suspicious game warden, I handed McKinney a beer and started asking him questions!

The crux of a lot of feet shuffling, rock kicking, all with head hung low was this. McKinney's archery hunt had only been partially successful. The successful part included the stalk and not much else. He'd hit the goat with what I call a "California Head Shot." I know this statement is not politically correct, but it is accurate. I will leave it to your imagination, as to where he actually hit the goat. Anyway, while some day light remained, McKinney headed out with his rifle to "get his goat" with the game warden's blessing.

Next morning I stopped by Mckinney's place on my way to work to check on his progress. Now if you like the look and smell of old goats, you would have liked this goat. I didn't! Now that McKinney had his goat the next question begged to be asked. (You don't know how sorry I was later that I did) "What are you going to do with it!?"

Come Saturday says he, we're going to have ourselves a Texas style BBQ! McKinney had already worked out the details. He'd BBQ the goat, all us single guys would bring chips and beer, and the only three single women in the county would bring themselves and a green salad. Could there be any better way to spend a September, Saturday afternoon?

After getting the goat and prior to the BBQ, McKinney told us all to have refreshed palates on Saturday because we'd surely all be delivered of ordinary BBQ once and for all! Anticipation ran high among us bachelors. With all three single women in the county attending, no matter what the virtues of BBQ as extolled by our friend from Texas, BBQ was way down the menu that Saturday afternoon.

Just as apple goes with pie, beer goes with BBQ! As we sipped cool malted beverages and waited for the women, McKinney regaled us with stories of past BBQ's in the great state of Texas. McKinney told us goats were second behind Longhorns as the national animal of Texas. The out put of our salivary glands increased with each story. This increased glandular activity peaked when a pickup pulled into the yard bearing all the single women of the county! Of the group, only I had observed McKinney's goat on the hoof, in his pickup, and now perched on a cutting board next to the BBQ grill.

With all invited guests in attendance, McKinney prepared to light charcoal to begin the BBQ. Let me digress here to explain how Texans do BBQ versus the way Yankees do BBQ. Yankees, as defined by Texans, are all those citizens of the United States of America who live north of San Antonio. Texans utilize a covered chamber with the meat on a grill, while the heat supplied by coals or charcoal is in an attached fire box. Their BBQ is slow cooked with this indirect heat and basted towards the end with BBQ sauce. On the other hand, Yankees place the meat directly over the coals and slop BBQ sauce on throughout the cooking process. To adequately impress all his new found Yankee friends, McKinney had rigged a genuine Texas BBQ. The main event was set to begin.

All of us were suitably impressed with McKinney's preparations although some expressed doubt about the "goat". Good beer, good conversation, and the thought of spending the afternoon with the only three single women in the county gave each of us the resolve to see the afternoon through! As McKinney jockeyed the coals around just right, the rest of us were jockeying for position with the women. To anyone driving or walking by, the scene appeared idyllic. Then McKinney began to apply heat to the hindquarters of this goat.

Though we in attendance, who by definition were Yankees, and had all expressed reservations about BBQ'd goat, none of us were prepared for what happened next! As smoke began to billow from the genuine Texas BBQ only a rapid evacuation prevented serious loss of life! McKinney, to this day maintains there was no toxicity associated with the smoke cloud which issued forth. This cloud hung close to the ground and only dissipated when the gusty winds of an afternoon thunderstorm threatened to take limbs off of nearby trees.

Except for exceptional circumstances one should never ridicule the cook! This event, if one can call it that, exceeded even "exceptional". All of us who cook know the terror of having dinner flop with guests already arriving. Things went from bad to worse for us all when all three single women in the county piled into their pickup truck and left. The smell of burning rubber from their tires was pleasant indeed, when compared to McKinney's goat not yet medium rare! Imagine if you can, the caustic comments of dinner guests forced to sit just downwind from a barrel full of smoldering gym shoes, discarded socks, and old saddle blankets!

Anyway...these many years later I've yet to taste my first BBQ'd goat!

GAME MEAT

Browsing through this section, one might think I've written a "Wild Game Cook Book". I confess, most of the meat recipes do feature "game" meat in this book. But, every "game" recipe easily converts to the cellophane wrapped meats found in your local meat market. Far be it from me to try converting those meat eaters who just don't like eating wild game, but read on to find out why I like it myself.

Any gardener will tell you his or her home grown produce tastes much better than any store bought veggies. By the same token, pull the lid off a Dutch oven full of BBQ elk ribs and I guarantee they'll put the store bought variety to shame. Whether it's putting sun dried tomatoes on the shelf or filling the freezer with lots of plain white packages marked "Elk Steak", nothing beats the fruits of one's own labors.

My love affair with game meat goes back to when I graduated from a high chair to a chair with pillows on it to boost me to appropriate height at the dinner table. Growing up in SE Idaho in the 50's and 60's dinner menus at the Welch household regularly featured venison along with beef, pork and lamb. Though not in a subsistence situation, venison and pheasants helped stretch the grocery dollars needed for a family of six.

Sitting here many years and many deer later, writing this book, I remember how proud I felt going home after getting my first deer. I know mom quickly got bored with my story but a thirteen year old helping Dad bring home the "bacon" just naturally gets a swelled chest. Over the intervening years I've not got an animal every year, but my freezer has never been empty of game meat thanks to other family members or my hunting pards!

Growing up, game meat was a staple on our table, as well as most of the neighbors. About the only folks I knew who didn't eat it were those few people who weren't hunters or fishermen. Like a lot of things from our childhoods, I just took game meat for granted.

My education about folks who didn't care for game meat began in college. My roommate and I asked a couple of gals over to our apartment for steaks one evening. They thought it would be neat to have a couple of guys cook them a steak dinner with all the trimmings. Both of us being from southern Idaho, just expected these gals to be suitably impressed not only with our culinary prowess, but with the fare as well. Wrong! One of these gals would have put a circus elephant to shame with her nose wrinkling ability when my roommate slapped those elk steaks on the grill. To make a long story short, they ate the trimmins' and we ate steak. Being some-what slow learners, both of us had to have this same lesson repeated just a month later with two different gals. In both cases we missed the clue of these gals coming from beyond the borders of "meat and tater" land! Rest assured though, this dislike of game meat is not gender specific.

After graduating from college and becoming a wildlife professional, I learned just how many people in our society don't hunt and have never had the opportunity to eat game meat. I've also met a lot of folks who've been served game meat and for various reasons didn't like it. Without first hand knowledge I wouldn't venture a guess as to "why" they didn't like game meat, but I can make some guesses based on my own experience.

Not only have I harvested numerous big game animals, but as a game warden I've been able to see how others take care of big game animals. By and large most folks do a pretty good job. Yet every year I see animals which, I've no doubt if you cooked a steak from, would gag a maggot! One of the worst instances I've encountered happened about ten years ago in the Little Lost Valley. It was mid morning on a Friday when I pulled into a camp to check a good size 6 x 6 bull elk.

These fellows had been luckier than most. They'd been able to load the bull whole into a truck. The cottonwood tree they picked to hang it from lacked a branch at the proper height, so they hung it from the next best branch which left the head, neck and one front shoulder still on the ground. One front quarter lacked any air circulation at all. The elk had been field dressed, but not skinned. The tag showed the bull had been killed on Wednesday. I asked the lucky hunter if he thought the carcass had cooled adequately. He replied "sure." Though the October nights had been down into the twenty degree range, the Indian Summer days were getting up to about sixty degrees.

When asked, the hunter had no objection to my taking a carcass temperature. I made a small slit in the hide and inserted a thermometer behind a shoulder blade. Thirty six hours after being killed the internal temperature was still over 60 degrees. Now, you tell me how many repeat customers a restaurant would get if they served beef given the same care?!? I'm not saying the quality of game meat totally reflects the care given in the field, but in my opinion it's a big first step.

Yet, still others are adamant a bull elk or a big buck taken in the rut borders on being inedible. My personal experience doesn't support this. A person who harvests such an animal might be wise to put more of it into burger and stew meat and plan to adjust the cooking of other cuts accordingly. To make my point, I pose this question to you, the reader. When fast food chains purchase cattle to be ground up for burgers, do they buy corn fed eighteen month old steers or old stringy, worn-out range bulls?

On occasion I've had the chance to serve some people their first taste of venison. Interestingly enough, most are pleasantly surprised, even those who may have previously had an unpleasant experience. Each different game animal will have a distinctive taste. There is no argument game meat differs in taste when compared to domestic meat. Not to be to "hoity toity" here, but having to acquire a taste for something different is not a new phenomenon. As for me, I'll take a nice elk steak over raw oysters any day!

I don't know exactly when the "lite food generation" began, but I'm sure it's here to stay. When we as a society started this long road to health awareness, it became obvious, though it had just three letters, "fat" was now a dirty word. With that realization society began to look towards game meat from a health perspective.

Published figures indicate game meat, on the average, contains less than 50% of the fat found in domestic animals. Even a well trimmed cut of meat from the grocery store yields more fat than the equivalent cut from a game animal due to the lack of "marbling" found in game meats. I've known individuals with heart problems who, on the advice of their doctors, limited their consumption of red meat to game meat.

This camp meal, prepared by Cee Dub, featured (clockwise from top left) Cee Dub's Basic Bisuits, Cee Dub's Fancy Veggies, Barbeque Ribs and the Leg of Lamb or Ram recipes.

Mike Robertson Photo

_____ Words of Wisdom _____

On pack trips or a raft trip plan your pork and poultry meals for the first few days, as they don't keep as well. Personally, I prefer to start dinner with pork or poultry still partially frozen rather than have either of them sitting in a cooler totally thawed out for a day or two.

DUTCH OVEN
__ELK RIB OR BRISKET BARBEQUE __

Ingredients:

1 12-inch cast iron Dutch oven
4 to 5 lbs. of charcoal
Charcoal lighter
1 metal garbage can lid or fire pan (even an old hub
 cap can be used as a fire pan)
Kitchen tongs, lid lifter
3 to 4 lbs. of boneless elk brisket or 3 to 4 lbs of elk
 ribs cut in 6 to 8 inch lengths
3 to 4 Tbsp. of cooking oil
3 to 4 cloves of garlic
1 to 2 cups of hearty burgundy wine
6 to 8 cans of beer (your choice)
2 medium onions

Trim and pat dry ribs or brisket; cut brisket into ½ to 1 lb. chunks.

Start 20 to 25 charcoal briquets. When briquets are well started, spread out half of them in the fire pan and set Dutch oven over them. Make sure the Dutch is level.

Add cooking oil to Dutch oven and press garlic cloves into the oil as it warms. Saute for 2 to 3 minutes.

Add meat, and turn frequently for a few minutes. Quarter or dice onions and arrange on top on meat.

Leave 1 inch of space on top. Add wine and six pack of beer. Put lid on and add remaining briquets to the lid with old kitchen tongs.

Be prepared to add more briquets in about 1 to 1 ½ hours after starting. Check occasionally and add more liquid if necessary.

Allow to simmer for 3 to 4 hours; 30 to 40 minutes before serving remove lid and pour off excess liquid leaving about ½ inch in bottom of Dutch oven. Brush on barbeque sauce, put lid back on and reduce number of briquets in half. Remove briquets about 10 minutes before serving. Serve with barbeque sauce on the side, green garden vegetables, potato salad and homemade rolls.

—————— BUTCH'S BBQ SAUCE ——————

Ingredients:

2 cups burgundy wine
½ cup red wine vinegar
2 to 3 Tbsp. cooking oil
2 to 3 Tbsp. Worcestershire® sauce or Heinz 57®
1 cup ketchup
½ cup chili sauce
1 tsp. Wrights'® liquid smoke
½ tsp. Tabasco®
1 Tbsp. ground horseradish

Combine the above in saucepan and stir together.

Add:
½ cup brown sugar
1 Tbsp. superfine ground mustard
1 Tbsp. each of thyme, oregano and paprika
½ Tbsp. coarse ground pepper
½ tsp. salt
½ tsp. Wrights'® liquid smoke.

Use a wire whisk to blend - simmer just below boiling to achieve desired consistency, 1 to 1 ½ hours, usually.

Add ketchup to thicken or more wine to thin. It will thicken as it cools.

LEG of RAM or LAMB

Not many of us ever get the chance to really get our fill of wild sheep meat, but every opportunity we have should be considered a treat.

Ingredients:

Leg of "ram" 5 - 8 lbs. If you bone it out, it will fit better in your 14" DO. A leg of lamb fits good in a 12" DO. (a deep one if you have it)

10 -12 cloves of garlic, slice half of them fairly thin
3 - 4 ribs of celery cut into 1" pieces (celery seed will do in camp)
1 large yellow onion
1 cup red wine (more if you need it)
½ cup water
fresh rosemary
ground thyme
Salt/pepper
¼ cup mint jelly if doing domestic lamb

Trim any excess fat, especially from a domestic lamb. Take a thin bladed knife and make cuts and insert garlic cloves. Rub your roast with a little olive oil then salt and pepper to taste. Place the Dutch oven over 10 -14 briquets and saute about half of your garlic slices. Lightly brown the roast 3 - 4 minutes per side. After you add the wine and water, sprinkle with fresh rosemary and just a dash of thyme. Add the celery and cover with onion slices. Cover tightly.

Use about equal number of briquets on the lid and cook for 1 ½ to 2 ½ hours depending on the size of your roast. If doing domestic lamb, spoon off ½ cup juice after an hour to mix with the mint jelly. Baste two or three times as roast cooks. Garnish with fresh rosemary just before serving.

Trim away any excess fat, make slits in the meat and insert garlic slices, rub with olive oil and seasonings.

Mike Robertson Photos

Saute about ½ of the garlic slices and sear the meat for 3 - 4 minutes on each side.

After you add wine and the water, sprinkle with fresh rosemary and a dash of thyme, add veggies and cover tightly.

LAMB SHANKS WITH GARLIC

Ingredients:

4 lamb shanks
1 bulb garlic, peel the cloves and slice length-wise
1 large onion-sliced
1 cup burgundy
1 cup water
olive oil
salt/pepper

Talk about a garlic lovers delight, this is it! I first tasted lamb shanks at the Overland Hotel, a small family style Basque restaurant in Gardnerville, Nevada. This is my version which, though delicious, probably doesn't quite compare with the original.

Place a 12" Dutch oven over 8 - 10 briquets and saute, until golden brown, about half the garlic. Salt and pepper the shanks if you wish. Brown the shanks two at a time for 4 - 5 minutes. Add the wine and water and sprinkle the remaining garlic over the top. Place the onion slices in the Dutch oven last. Put the lid on and use 14 - 16 briquets on the top. Cook for about two hours. Serve on a warmed plate if possible.

Use a slotted spoon to scoop up additional garlic and onions as a garnish.

Serves four as a main dish or 6-8 as an appetizer

Words of Wisdom

When cooking with cast iron, start with the pan and oil pre-heated to keep stuff from sticking.

Ingredients:

ROSEMARY

Elk Rump Roast 5-7 lbs.
4 - 6 Cloves of Garlic diced/sliced thin
2 - 3 lbs. small red potatoes
2 lbs. carrots scrubbed and sliced
    diagonally in 1" chunks
1- 2 medium onions quartered
1 cup burgundy (more if you need it)
1 cup water or soup stock
1 bunch parsley
olive oil
salt/pepper
2 - 3 Tbsp. fresh rosemary

Place a 14" Dutch oven over 8 - 10 briquets and add ¼ cup olive oil. Salt and pepper or season the roast to taste. Saute garlic and then lightly brown the roast on all sides. Add the wine and soup stock to the Dutch oven along with half the onions. Sprinkle part of the rosemary over the roast. Place 14 - 16 briquets on the lid and cook for 30 - 45 minutes. At this point check your liquid. There should be at least 1-2 inches around the roast. Add water if needed. Place the carrots and potatoes around the roast and continue cooking for another 30 - 40 minutes. Be ready to add more charcoal if your coals begin to look too puny. I like onions only slightly cooked so, I'll add the rest of my onions and sprinkle with the rest of the rosemary about fifteen minutes before I take the roast off the heat. Your roast should be medium to well done after 1½ - 2 hours. Decrease cooking time accordingly for a rare to medium rare roast. Pull the roast out of the Dutch oven and let rest for a few minutes before slicing. Serve the vegetables right from the Dutch oven and spoon the liquid over the meat and veggies.

Serves 6 - 8

___ MIDDLE FORK SPARERIBS ___

I spent from late 1978 through mid 1987 patrolling the Middle Fork of Salmon River. When I first put in for a transfer to this patrol area, I was told it meant becoming a "white water boatman"!

Up to this point, my only experience in command of a boat of any sort was a canoe at Boy Scout Camp getting across a mill pond!

To say I was a reluctant student would be an understatement of the first magnitude. By my own admission, the learning curve appeared extremely steep. Rather than bore you with harrowing tales of flipped rafts and gaping holes torn in rafts, I'll share a description with you from the other officer who "taught" me the river! He described my attempts with the oars as reminding him of a "daddy long legs spider suffering from a near fatal dose of a banned pesticide"! No longer do I have to put up with such verbal abuse. Now, years later, I'm able to show up on a river trip without embarrassing myself or the outfit I work for.

Cee Dub takes a well earned rest after a day on the Middle Fork of the Salmon, before fixin' a Dutch oven feast.

Dan Miller Photo

While running the Middle Fork of Salmon River, one of the outstanding white water rivers in the lower forty eight, I realized just how much this type of wilderness experience can mean to folks from across the nation and for that matter across the world. River outfitters realized the cuisine offered on their trips often left their guests in awe just as much as the other elements of the trip.

Many of the recipes in this book have been shared with me by river guides and other private boaters. Tony Latham, formerly a river guide and now a game warden for IDFG, shared this recipe with me several years ago.

——— MIDDLE FORK SPARERIBS ———

Ingredients:

4 - 5 lbs. spareribs
½ cup vinegar
1 can of beer
Salt/pepper/seasonings
Barbeque Sauce
Water

Parboil spareribs in a 12" DO in water & vinegar for 20 - 30 minutes. Drain water and rendered fat off and pat the ribs dry with a paper towel. Season with salt/pepper and your favorite seasonings. (I like to use a little garlic salt in lieu of regular salt. For an oriental flavor use a little Chinese Five Spice.)

At this point, brush the ribs with barbeque sauce and season to taste. Place the ribs in the Dutch and add the can of beer, reserving the last swig for the cook. Put the DO in the firepan with 8 - 10 briquets top and bottom.
Bake for 30 - 45 minutes.   Serves 4 - 6

Tony Latham, IDF&G

DUTCH OVEN
BARBEQUE BRISKET

Ingredients:

5 - 7 lbs. boneless beef brisket
(Elk or Moose will do, too.)
1 - 2 large slicing onions
3 - 4 cloves of garlic (Mashed or sliced)
2 bottles of beer
½ cup BBQ Sauce
¼ cup olive oil
salt/pepper/seasonings

Trim as much fat as possible off the brisket and trim to fit in a 12" DO. Rub with a small amount of oil and salt and pepper to taste. Saute garlic in oil till golden brown. Place brisket in DO, sear 3 - 4 minutes per side. At this point I like to sprinkle the brisket liberally with Schillings Chicken Mesquite Seasoning®. Cover with sliced onions and add beer. If yours is a "dry camp" substitute 4 - 5 cups water and or beef bouillon.

Put about the same number of briquets top and bottom, 12 -14, and for the next hour work on shucking the corn or putting the finishing touches on a potato salad. Check the liquid about this time and add more if needed. Keep about 1" liquid in your DO.

Minimum cooking time is about 1½ hours. I prefer to cook mine about twice that long, which is usually enough to make this fairly tough cut of meat succulent and tender. Add fresh charcoal when needed. Forty-five minutes before dinner pull the lid and brush top side with BBQ sauce and continue to cook for 30 minutes.

Fifteen minutes before serving, remove brisket from DO and allow to rest on a cutting board. Slice and serve with your favorite BBQ sauce on the side. (Only Yankees eat their meat smothered with BBQ sauce)   Serves 8-10.

BARBEQUED SPARERIBS

This recipe goes back to the 1940's and was gleaned from a cookbook written, published and distributed by the women of the Soda Springs, Idaho, Presbyterian Church. We could reprint the whole cookbook and have a best seller, but we chose Mike's mother's and aunt's spareribs. Just don't tell them that we gave out the recipe. This was written for oven cooking, but works great in a Dutch.

Preheat oven to 350 degrees (prepare coals for DO).

Ingredients:

4 lbs. spareribs
1 large onion cut fine
2 Tbsp. butter
2 Tbsp. vinegar
4 Tbsp. lemon juice
1 Tbsp. brown sugar
1/8 tsp. cayenne pepper
1 cup catsup or tomato soup
3 tsp. Worchestershire sauce
1/2 tsp. ground mustard
1 cup water
1/2 cup diced celery or 1 Tbsp. celery salt (if desired)
1 garlic bud, diced
2 Tbsp. fat

Brown spareribs in cast iron skillet using fat. When brown on both sides, remove spareribs to DO. Melt butter and brown onions in cast iron skillet and add remainder of ingredients, stir and pour over ribs in DO.

Cook in DO until ribs are tender.   Serves 4 to 6

Thanks to Isabel Robertson and Alice Tigert

__ SHORT RIBS with DUMPLINGS __

Ingredients:

3 - 4 lbs. of elk/moose/beef short ribs
(cut boneless plate or brisket in 2" chunks)
2 - 3 onions cut in wedges
6 - 8 carrots scrubbed and cut in 1" chunks
2 - 3 Idaho taters cut in quarters
4 - 5 bay leaves
3 - 4 cloves of garlic, sliced thin
2 - 3 cups of water/beef stock or beer
olive oil
salt/pepper and/or any other seasoning you wish

This works best in a deep 12" or 14" DO which gives your
dumplings room to fluff up. Season the meat to taste while
you saute the garlic. Add the meat and fry for 5 -10 minutes,
stirring several times. Put in about half the onion wedges
and bay leaves when you pour the cooking liquid in. Set the
DO in your firepan over 12 - 14 briquets and let simmer for a
couple of hours. Since you're using a fairly tough cut of
meat, the longer you cook it, the easier it will be on the
older folks' dentures. Add the remaining onions, vegetables,
more liquid if needed, and cook for 20 minutes while you
mix your dumplings.* Spoon the dumplings in with a large
kitchen spoon, cover and let simmer for another 20 minutes.
(The horseradish dumplings go great with this)

Serves 4 - 6

* See page 71 • Basic Biscuit Recipe for Dumplings

Words of Wisdom

When shopping, look for firm,
well-shaped onions with
unblemished, papery skins. Peel
onions under running cold water
to prevent eyes from watering.

—————— LIVER and ONIONS ——————

Ingredients:

Deer or elk liver, sliced ¼" thick (enough to serve 4 - 5)
3 - 4 medium size onions, sliced
3 - 4 Tbsp. cooking oil

Soak liver overnight in cold water. Heat oil in large cast-iron skillet. Add liver slices and season to taste with pepper and garlic salt. Turn liver in 3 - 4 minutes. Cover with onion slices. Cover and cook for 5 minutes. Stir once or twice and then serve.
Note: Sliced heart can be substituted. Also, some like to dredge liver slices in flour before frying.

—————— SWISS STEAK ——————

Ingredients:

Round Steak - beef, elk, venison, buffalo, etc.
Bell pepper - diced or sliced
Diced onion
Mushrooms
Tomato Sauce
Salt, Pepper, Garlic Powder

Rub meat with flour, salt , pepper, and garlic powder. Pound this into meat then brown slightly on both sides. Place meat in DO, put peppers, mushrooms and onions on meat and then cover with tomato sauce.

Amount of each used depends on the amount of meat used. Cook until meat is tender and sauce thickens. (45 minutes to 1 hour)

Mike McLain, Colorado Division of Wildlife

BAKED ELK HEART
with SAGE DRESSING

Soak elk heart overnight in cold water. Simmer in large kettle for 1 to 1½ hours. Season broth to taste with garlic powder, pepper and bay leaves, plus 1 small diced onion may be used. Pour off and retain all but about ½ cups of broth.

Ingredients:

2 boxes prepared dressing mix
1 tsp. sage
2 Tbsp. margarine

In large bowl, combine dressing mix and add sage. Heat to boiling the stock poured off heart and add margarine. Use just enough broth to thoroughly moisten dressing. Spoon dressing around heart in a baking dish or DO and bake for 1½ - 2 hours at 350 degrees.

When done, slice heart ¼" to ½" thick and serve hot. (Leftovers make good sandwiches.)

Note: If you like homemade dressing, try this instead of a prepared mix.

Ingredients:

10 cups stale bread, diced
1 medium sized onion, diced
1- 2 cups sliced celery
1 Tbsp. sage

Mix ingredients and prepare as for boxed dressing.

Serves 4.

MIKE'S DUTCH OVEN BARBEQUE
———————PORK RIB DINNER ———————

Ingredients:

4 lbs. boneless country style pork ribs
2 medium size yellow or white onions
1 clove fresh garlic
½ lb. fresh whole mushrooms
3 large Idaho Russet potatoes
½ lb. fresh carrots
2 large yellow or red peppers
Bottle inexpensive red wine
Onion salt, pepper, Mrs. Dash®
1 bottle barbeque sauce
   (or see page 89 for Butch's BBQ sauce)
⅓ cup Canola or olive oil
1 12" DO
24 to 30 charcoal briquets

Start half of the briquets while preparing ingredients for the DO. Make sure that all ingredients are at room temperature— not cold or frozen. Slowly heat DO over camp stove with oil spread evenly in bottom.

Season pork with spices as DO is warming. Add pork and brown on all sides in heated DO. Once browned, place DO over hot coals and thoroughly cover with barbeque sauce. Add about 1 cup wine. Add vegetables in layers starting with onions and garlic. Finish with potatoes, peppers and whole mushrooms. Place lid on Dutch and add 8 to 10 briquets on top of Dutch lid. Cook 2 to 2½ hours, adding cooking liquid about every one half hour.

Serves 6 to 8, depending on how hungry the crew.

Mike Robertson
Twin Falls, ID

⸺ GAME WARDEN SCRAMBLE ⸺

A recipe guaranteed not to make friends and influence enemies, especially if they happen to be a game warden.

Ingredients:

1 local rancher
1 domestic goat
1 subject (?)
1 nearsighted informant
1 excited game warden
1 search warrant
1 wasted day
1 egg

Start with the local rancher giving a domestic goat to a subject. Have the subject skin the goat in his yard. Stir in a nearsighted informant who sees the subject skinning the goat.

Have the informant find the game warden and advise him of subject skinning a *deer*. Let the excited game warden stew for 4 hours waiting for search warrant.

Once game warden has received a search warrant and is thoroughly stewed, let him serve it on subject and find goat.

Mix all together and you have a wasted day. Put egg on game warden's face.

Thought for the day. "A game warden can always be relied upon to waste a day trying to get your goat."

Wyoming Game Warden's Association

Favorite Camp Meals

HEARTY DUTCH OVEN BREAKFAST

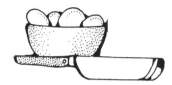

Ingredients:

1 lb. ground venison
2 Tbsp. vegetable oil
1 small onion, diced

Brown ground venison in vegetable oil with onion and season to taste. Pour off any excess grease.

1 dozen eggs
1 can diced jalapenos (small)
 Use green chilies if you like it mild
1 lb. medium or sharp Cheddar cheese
 (Monterey Jack or Swiss can be substituted)

Break eggs and add diced jalapenos to cooked meat. Stir over medium heat until eggs are nearly cooked. Sprinkle cheese over top. Remove from heat and let sit for 2 - 3 minutes. Serve with salsa or sour cream.

Serves 4 - 6.

Words of Wisdom

Do not rinse canned chilies since much of the taste will go down the drain with the water. If they are packed in vinegar, they may be rinsed.

A can or two of black olives in the chuck box can be used to add color and a little flavor to any number of dishes.

DUTCH OVEN OMELETTE

This easy recipe isn't really a true omelette, but was called such by one of the patrons on a Selway River whitewater trip I was cookin' for one rainy summer week. The name stuck and has been a favorite since.

To be honest, there is no set ingredients list. The "omelette" seems to change all the time, depending upon what we have on hand in camp.

Ingredients:
   (subject to change- depends on what you have)

2 dozen X-large eggs
2 cups cubed ham or pork, crumbled bacon strips, country sausage, sausage link pieces or left over steak from the night before (or some of, and/or all the above).
1 cup each diced onions & bell peppers (green, yellow, red)
1 cup sliced mushrooms
1 to 2 chopped fresh tomatoes
2 cups shredded cheddar cheese
Spices - salt, pepper, Mrs. Dash® and Tobasco®
1 cup milk
1 stick butter (melted)
½ cup canola or olive oil

Coat inside of Dutch with oil. Break eggs into Dutch, add milk and whip until thoroughly mixed. Stir in the rest of ingredients, except one cup of cheese. Cover and place on heat source. This meal is best cooked over a camp stove or firebox for better temperature control. Low and slow is best.

In initial phase of cooking, stir frequently as eggs start to cook. As eggs set up with cooking, lower heat until fully cooked. In last few minutes before serving, spread last cup of shredded cheese over omelette, replace lid and let melt.

Mike Robertson, Twin Falls, ID   Serves 10 to 12

___ GARDEN VEGETABLE EGGS ___

A skillet breakfast that will bring everybody back for seconds. Be ready to cook plenty.

Ingredients:

3 Tbsp. margarine or butter
2 cups thinly sliced zucchini
1 cup sliced fresh mushrooms
1 medium onion, thinly sliced
2 medium tomatoes cut into wedges (2 cups)
½ tsp. basil leaves
Salt and pepper to taste
12 eggs
¼ cup water
2 Tbsp. margarine or butter for eggs

In a large cast iron skillet or dutch oven, melt 3 tablespoons of margarine (butter), add zucchini, mushrooms & onion; saute over medium heat until crisp/tender. Add tomatoes and ½ teaspoon basil. Cover and cook for one to two minutes or until tomatoes are thoroughly heated. Remove from heat.

Salt and pepper to taste. Arrange on serving platter, cover and keep warm.

At the same time, scramble eggs in two tablespoons of margarine or butter. Spoon over cooked veggies and sprinkle with basil. Serve immediately.

Serves 6 to 8.

Tricia Robertson
Caldwell, ID

BREAKFAST MEATS
DUTCH OVEN STYLE

When cooking breakfast for a large group of folks, don't waste valuable cooking area by fixing bacon, sausage or other breakfast meat in a fry pan over your stove.

Use the Dutch in your fire pit, or in the firebox if you are restricted to use of such a box on the river or camping.

Ingredients:

1 to 2 lbs. of bacon, depending on number of people. Ham, link or Italian sausage, pork loin or all the above.

12" or 14" Dutch Oven.

Place meats - bacon first - in bottom of Dutch. Put any or all of the other miscellaneous meats over the top of the bacon.

Cover Dutch and put in fire pit or firebox over and against hot wood coals.

As the meat cooks and "fry's up," stir frequently to keep from burning. When done, pull from fire and transfer breakfast meats to deep dish or pan lined with paper towels to absorb any fat not drained on transfer from Dutch.

Serves a bunch! Figure one fourth pound per person.

Mike Robertson
Twin Falls, ID

DUTCH OVEN LASAGNA

Ingredients:

½ lb. Italian sausage
½ lb. lean burger (elk or beef)
4 - 6 cloves of garlic minced
1 small onion minced
1 jar (28 - 30 oz.) of spaghetti sauce
   (Try the Super Mushroom)
1 18 - 20 oz. container of ricotta cheese
1 box of lasagna noodles
1 cup grated Parmesan cheese
2 cups grated mozzarella cheese
2 cups grated cheddar cheese
4 - 5 Tbsp. parsley, chopped coarse
Olive oil
Italian seasoning (Fresh herbs are best
   if you have them.)
Salt/pepper

If you only have one DO in camp you'll need another good size pan to prepare the sauce in, plus a kettle to boil the pasta in. Start by setting a DO in the firepan over 8 - 10 briquets or on the camp stove over medium heat.

With 2 - 3 tablespoons of olive oil saute the garlic and onions for 4 - 5 minutes then add the meat and brown. Pour off any excess fat before you pour in the spaghetti sauce. Season to taste and simmer for 15 - 20 minutes while you grate the cheese. To speed things up, have a pot of water heating to cook the pasta in. Cook according to package directions.

While the pasta is cooking stir the parsley into the ricotta cheese. Place a thin layer of the meat sauce in the bottom of a 12" DO and spread it evenly. Next put in a layer of lasagna noodles and mozzarella and ricotta cheese topped with another layer of the meat sauce. You should have enough for 4 - 5 layers. After the last layer, top with half of the cheddar cheese. Put the lid on the DO and set it in the fire pan over 6 - 8 briquets. Bake with 16 - 18 briquets on the lid for 40 - 45 minutes or until you just can't take the smell any longer.

When you take it out of the firepan, lift the lid and sprinkle the remaining cheddar cheese over the top. Let it set for a few minutes then serve with parmesan.

A great dinner for the Soudough French Bread heated in a Dutch.

Serves 6-8

Cindi A. Ferro
Moscow, ID

Words of Wisdom _____

Carry a small bottle of chlorine bleach. After you rinse your dishes, rinse them in a second cool rinse to which you've added one cap full of bleach for two gallons of water.

Before you toss the dish water after doing the dishes, strain the dish water and put the solid waste in your garbage to be packed out.

When you toss the dish water, try to get more than two steps from the tent and don't throw it where someone is going to step in it.

——— COOKING from CANS ———

There are times when cooking in camp means cooking with canned and/or dried food. In 1991, one of my rafting pards lucked out and drew a permit for the Grand Canyon. Our plan to cover the 226 miles over eighteen days necessitated planning meals beyond when grub, frozen in coolers, would last. Summer temperatures seem to hover in the upper 90's on the Colorado River in June. In our "Cook for the Day" lottery, I drew days 3, 8, and 16.

Day 3's menu featured all fresh ingredients and by using dry ice, I was able to use frozen items for Day 8. In planning my meals for Day 16, my only choices were dried and canned ingredients. Here is my dinner menu for Day 16!

——— SAND BAR PASTA SALAD———

Ingredients:

2 pkgs,12 oz. each of vegtable Rotelli
2 regular size cans of pitted black olives, sliced
1 can, 15 oz. of garbonzo beans, drained
1 can, 15 oz. of red kidney beans, drained
2 cans, 4 oz. each of diced pimentos drained
¼ cup red wine vinegar
½ cup olive oil
1 Tbsp. each of dried minced onion and garlic.
Salt/pepper

While cooking the pasta according to package directions, I added the minced onion and garlic to the olive oil/wine vinegar. When the pasta finsihed, I drained it and added the remaining ingredients.

After tossing to mix, I set the DOs in an empty cooler in 4 - 5 inches of river water. (With 48 - 50 degree water temperature the salad cooled quite well in about an hour.)

Serves 16

TANGY GLAZED HAMS

Ingredients: per 12" DO

3 boneless canned hams - 2 lb. each
1 bottle, 2 oz. of maraschino cherries
1 can, 15 oz. of pineapple rings
1 cup water
Glaze
1 jar, 8 oz. of orange marmalade
½ tsp. Tabasco® or other hot pepper sauce
6 oz. Amaretto

Mix the glaze ingredients together and let set while you're getting the charcoal ready. Place the hams in the DO along with juices from the cans. Brush each ham with the glaze and any other seasoning you wish to add. Place pineapple rings on each ham with a maraschino cherry in the center of each ring. Set the DO in a firepan with 8 - 10 briquets underneath and 12 - 14 around the outside of the lid and cook for an hour. Brush each ham with the remaining glaze 2 - 3 times.

CANNED YAMS for HAM

Ingredients: per 12" DO

2 cans, 28 oz. each of sliced sweet potatoes, drained
1 can, 4 oz. of crushed pineapple with juice
¼ cup brown sugar
½ cup water
¼ cup of squeeze bottle margarine
Salt/pepper or your favorite seasoning

Put water in your DO and arrange sliced yams in layers. Season to taste, then squeeze margarine over the top. Spoon in the crushed pineapple and sprinkle with brown sugar. Set the DO in the firepan with 12 - 14 briquets on top and bottom for 30 minutes.   Serves 8

HOWARD'S
REFRIED BEANS

Many of us, myself included, learn better when shown something versus reading about it and then trying to duplicate a particular dish or create it by reverse engineering. Such is the case with refried beans. For years I simply picked the appropriate size of can whenever refrieds were part of my menu. My pard, Howard Konetzke, Jr., from LaGrange, Texas, furthered my camp cooking education when he showed me how to make this recipe while visiting him a few years ago. Howard makes a **"BIG POT"** of beans and uses them as a side dish for everything for however long they last! When he gets down to the bottom of the **"BIG POT"** he makes a batch of refrieds. For traditional refrieds make them with butter or lard. For 'vegetarian refrieds' cook your beans without the ham hocks and use margarine or a little olive oil to make your refrieds!

Ingredients:
1 cup beans, pinto or Anasazi
1 ham hock
1 yellow onion, chopped
6 cloves garlic, minced
Salt and pepper to taste
Butter or margarine

If using pinto beans, soak overnight before cooking. Put beans in 12" Dutch oven with other ingredients. Add liquid to cover ham hock and simmer several hours until the meat cooks off the bone and beans are tender. Remove all the pieces of meat, skins and the bones of the ham hock. Continue to cook the liquid off the beans. Chop up the meat from the ham hock and add back into the beans and continue to reduce the liquid. Mash the beans and meat with a potato masher to a pasty consistency. Melt a few tablespoons of butter or margarine in a fry pan. Transfer bean and meat mixture to fry pan and continue to reduce the liquid by frying until the desired consistency of refried beans.

In lieu of making homemade refried beans, use canned refried beans and heat up in a small DO by melting a few tablespoons of butter or margarine and frying the beans to enhance the flavor.

KRAUT and DOGS

Ingredients:

1 chunk of salt pork, finely diced
Several cloves of garlic, minced
2 medium onions , minced
Butter, margarine or olive oil
2 cans, or equivalent, sauerkraut
1 package of German or Polish sausage
1 beer, or water
Pepper to taste

Wash the sauerkraut thoroughly in a colander with hot water to remove the sour taste. Place the washed sauerkraut in a DO with the beer or liquid. Saute the salt pork, garlic and onions in butter, margarine or olive oil until nearly cooked. Add to the sauerkraut. Slice the sausages into bite sized pieces and add to the kraut. Cover and simmer. The longer it simmers, the better it gets.

As an additional camp treat, do this—

Choose your favorite frozen fruit pie from the grocery freezer. Place a round baking rack in the bottom of a 12" Dutch oven. Place the frozen pie on the rack. Bake for 45-50 minutes or according to the instructions on the box using about 4 briquets on the bottom and 14-16 on the lid.

Words of Wisdom

In a dry camp, you can use the last of your coffee to do your dishes. It's already heated and it will cut dried egg yolk off a tin plate.

ELK n' KRAUT

Ingredients:

3 Idaho spuds, diced
1 ½ lbs. elk burger
1 cup water
2 tsp. salt
1 tsp. pepper
1 egg, beaten
2 Tbsp. catsup, chili sauce or barbeque sauce
1 jar Claussen® brand sauerkraut, drained
2 slices wheat bread, diced or 1 cup croutons
1 chopped onion
2 Tbsp. brown sugar
4 - 6 cheese slices

Heat oil in 12" Dutch oven. Add all the ingredients, except the cheese and stir once. Put on the lid and don't peek for 1 ½ hours. If cooking over a campfire, be careful not to put too many coals under the oven or food will stick. When done, remove from heat, add thin slices of cheese and let sit with lid on for one more minute. Enjoy.

Serves 4

Kent Ball, Sr.
IDFG Fishery Research Biologist
Region 6, Salmon, ID

Fowl & Fish

BROTHER-IN-LAW DUCK

This recipe will also work on mothers-in-law, if you can get them to shut up long enough to eat it.

Ingredients:

1 mud duck, partially cleaned. Preferably taken
    from a sewer lagoon.
1 can beer
1 cup castor oil
2 cups styrofoam packing material
1 small sagebrush, finely chopped
8 oz. spinach (for green slimy texture)
Broccoli - optional if George Bush is your brother-in-law,
    or any other disgusting ingredient you can think of
Salt and pepper to taste.

Throw the mud duck in a roaster that was last cleaned out by your hound dog. Mix all of the ingredients, except caster oil and beer. Stuff the duck with this mixture. Give the duck a good dose of castor oil and then pour beer over all. (Beer is very important since brothers-in-law go into a frenzy when they smell it.) Cook in oven on low heat for 1 hour. Garnish and serve piping hot.

If this does not stop your brother-in-law from coming to your house and drinking up all of your beer or asking for seconds or thirds, there is only one sure ingredient that you can add next time. It is illegal and you may have to do some time for it, but it probably would be worth it. Add ARSENIC! LOTS OF ARSENIC!!

Wyoming Game Warden's Association

DUTCH OVEN
—WILD DUCK or GOOSE in GRAVY—

Make this for people who always hated duck or goose — they will love it!

Ingredients:

2 ducks or 1 goose
Lard or shortening
Flour
Water
Salt
Pepper

Lightly salt and pepper inside of bird(s). Roll in flour to coat. Slowly brown bird(s) on all sides. Remove bird(s) to Dutch oven. Add flour to pan drippings. Cook and stir until brown. Add water, salt and pepper. Cook and stir until thickened. I usually make 4 - 5 cups of gravy.

1 small apple, quartered
1 potato chunked
1 onion, quartered
6 - 7 potatoes, cut up
1 - 2 onions, quartered

Stuff cavities with apple, onion, and chunked potato. Put remaining potatoes and onions around bird(s). Pour gravy over all. Bake slowly for 3 ½ to 4 hours or until meat is falling off the bones—tender and moist. Serve ½ duck to each person or slice of goose meat. Pass the potatoes and gravy. Serves 4.

Kim Wright, IDFG Conservation Officer, Region 3, Boise

ROAST DUCK in a DUTCH

Ingredients:

3 Ducks-whole & plucked (mallards/pintails)
5 small onions
2 apples (I prefer a tart variety)
3 - 4 ribs of celery cut in 1" pieces
6 - 8 carrots scrubbed and cut in 1" chunks
3 - 4 bay leaves
1 cup burgundy
1 cup chicken or duck stock
1 cup water
$\frac{1}{3}$ cup red currant preserves
6 slices of fresh side pork
Olive oil
Salt/pepper
Ground thyme

Wash ducks and pat dry inside and out. Rub each with a small amount of olive oil and stuff with an onion each and $\frac{1}{3}$ of an apple. Season to taste with salt and pepper or seasonings of your choice.

Arrange ducks in your Dutch and add about ½ cup each of wine and soup stock along with the bay leaves. Mix the currant preserves with ½ cup of the stock and brush each bird liberally. Put the carrots and celery around the birds and place two pieces of fresh side pork with a little ground thyme rubbed into it on each bird.

Cook for 1½ hours with 8 - 10 briquets on the bottom and 16 - 18 arranged around the outside of the lid.

Serves three as a main dish and 6 - 8 as an appetizer.

ALMOND DUCK
with
—— MANDARIN ORANGES ——
(Also Works Well With Chukar)

Ingredients:

½ cup raisins
2 oz. red wine
2 tsp. paprika
1 tsp. white pepper
2 ducks, boned & cut into
    bite-sized pieces
5 Tbsp. oil
1 can, 11 oz. mandarin
    oranges, drained, save juice
1 clove garlic

½ cup hot beef bouillon
1 Tbsp. cornstarch
1 Tbsp. soy sauce
½ tsp. powdered ginger
    (or 1 tsp. fresh
    grated ginger root)
½ cup evaporated milk
1 Tbsp. butter
2 Tbsp. sliced almonds or
    cashews

Soak raisins in wine. Toss duck pieces in paprika & pepper and brown in oil about 10 minutes. Pour ½ cup of mandarin orange juice over duck and add garlic & bouillon; cover and simmer.

Drain raisins and add to duck; cook 5 minutes. Blend cornstarch in small amount of cold water & add to duck and sauce, stir until thick & bubbly. Add soy sauce, ginger, oranges & evaporated milk; heat, but do not boil.

Saute almonds in butter in small iron skillet until golden. Sprinkle almonds over duck. Serve on steamed rice. Serves 6.

Phyillis Kochert
Office Coordinator, IDF&G
Boise, ID

HUNGRY RIDGE CHICKEN

Several years ago a bunch of us decided to try our hand at hunting white tail deer. To say we didn't know what we were getting into would be an understatement. (Having hunted mule deer all our lives, it almost seemed like cheating on the deer's part when all one ever seemed to see of a white tail deer was a white tail.) Anyway... we loaded a camp and headed for the Clearwater River country. Not knowing exactly where we were going kinda added to the sense of adventure.

According to the map, we ended up on "Hungry Ridge." I'm sure a story exists to explain that name, but our grub box contained enough food to where we wouldn't have to worry much about prolonged hunger. If you want to see what, "Hungry" in a hunting camp looks like, look up "Hungry" in the dictionary and you'll see a picture of three hungry game wardens coming through the flaps of my wall tent! Anyway....

Inside Cee Dub's wall tent... you can see there's not much room for "hungry" game wardens to come crashin' in.

C.W. Welch Photo Collection

120

A lot of recipes are born when the camp cook gets in a hurry and just starts throwing things together! Though I'm sure we weren't the first group of guys to camp there and call their dinner "Hungry Ridge Chicken", this recipe came to be under such circumstances.

—— HUNGRY RIDGE CHICKEN ——

Ingredients:

1 - 2 boneless chicken breasts per hunter
6 - 8 cloves of garlic
Olive oil
2 cans of beer
1 pkg. - 12 oz. wide egg noodles
1 26 oz. family-size can cream soup-mushroom,
    celery, or chicken
Salt/pepper & seasonings

Mash up the garlic and saute it in 3 - 4 tablespoons olive oil. Season the chicken breasts and saute for 4 - 5 minutes turning once. Add the beer (or the equivalent of water or chicken stock) and place in the DO. Place 10-15 briquets underneath and allow to cook for 30-40 minutes. Cook the noodles according to package directions but halve the cooking time. Drain and reserve excess water.

Pull the lid off the DO and spoon in the noodles and pour the soup over top. Return to the coals and continue cooking for 15-20 minutes. Add 1 - 2 cups of water reserved from noodles if original liquid has cooked off. This will keep the bottom from scorching.

Serves 6 - 8 depending on how hungry they are.

CAMP ROBERTSON QUICK-FIX
—— DUTCH OVEN CHICKEN ——

Quick-fix Dutch oven chicken is one of those one pot meals that doesn't take much time, but tastes like you spent hours getting it ready to impress friends, family or even in-laws. This is one that you can vary with ingredients you happen to have in the cooler at camp, or in the refrigerator at home. The first time I fixed this recipe, it was just sort of thrown together as a back-up to another Dutch entree for some folks who didn't enjoy the kind of red meat that was in it.

It turns out that that everybody enjoyed some of both and a new "main" entree became part of our camp menu. It works just as well in the back yard, or in the oven.

Ingredients:

8 to 12 fryer chicken pieces
Salt and Pepper
Garlic Pepper
Mrs. Dash®
12 small/medium red potatoes
2 large onions
1 to 2 lbs. carrots
¾ cup vegetable oil
2 cups medium-dry white wine
12" Dutch
24 - 30 charcoal briquets

Wash the chicken thoroughly and pat dry with paper towels. Season each side of chicken pieces with onion salt, pepper and garlic pepper. Layer in a bowl and season all pieces in layer with Mrs. Dash®. Once all the pieces are seasoned and layered, cover and set aside while preparing vegetables.

Scrub vegetables with a brush. Cut carrots into two to three inch pieces and onions into eighths. Many stores have prepared carrots in a bag. These work great and make the preparation time even quicker. Leave the red pototoes whole.

Using ½ of the briquets under the Dutch, brown chicken pieces in the oil, 4 pieces at a time, until crisp on outside. Layer chicken in bottom of Dutch, followed by onions, potatos and carrots. Pour wine over mixture and cover. Place remaining hot briquets on Dutch lid. Cook for 60 to 90 minutes, depending upon outside temperature.

Serves 6 to 8.

Mike Robertson
Twin Falls, ID

_____Words of Wisdom_____

If camping in an area where bears have been habituated to humans, a clean camp is an absolute must. This means dishes done after every meal, garbage kept to a minimum and stored out of reach and out of camp, and any food containers or coolers kept securely closed or hung in trees out of camp.

Being nocturnal for the most part, bears are more likely to come prowling once you hit the bed ground. Leave a couple of pots and pans or some cleaned out cans on the ground outside of camp. If a bear comes calling he'll typically rattle these around, giving you some warning he's in the area.

Don't try to fight a bear over food, or anything else for that matter. Even a little bear is tougher than you! The key to "bear less" camps is to make sure if a bear does show up, he is in no way rewarded.

LIB'S DUTCH OVEN CHICKEN
___BREASTS with FRESH CHILES___

Ingredients:

6 chicken breasts, boned
6 chili peppers, fresh
1 package peas, frozen
1 package baby lima beans, frozen
   (Don't tell Cee Dub!)
1 can mushroom pieces
1 can corn
1 can tomatoes
2 packages Lipton® Spanish Rice

Split, clean and wash chiles. Use mild Anahiem or hot
Serrano chiles per your taste.

Mix peas, lima beans, corn, mushrooms (drained), tomatoes
with juice with the Lipton's® Spanish Rice. Add enough water
to supplement liquid needed for rice. This mixture can be
mixed in a greased 12" DO.

Lay the fresh chiles on top of the above mixture. Place
seasoned chicken breasts on top of chiles/mixture.

Bake one hour at 350 degrees - 375 degrees or until
chicken is browned.

Margaritas or a white table wine goes well with this dinner.

Serves 4.

Libbi Graham
Game Warden
Utah Fish & Game

CARLSON RANCH SAGE CHICKEN

In the Upper Pahsimeroi Valley of Central Idaho, the old Carlson Ranch homestead provided my favorite camp spot to patrol out of for antelope hunters. With grouse season opening prior to antelope, I usually could round up a limit of sage grouse or a mix of sage and blue grouse to take to Carlson Ranch. Normally, we would pull a couple extra officers in for the antelope opener and by my second year in the Challis Patrol Area this dish became a tradition.

Ingredients:

3 sage grouse cut in quarters
3 - 4 onions cut in wedges
3 - 4 cans of beer (water/chicken stock if you've run
    out of beer)
3 - 4 cloves of garlic minced
1 can of mushroom soup
1 can cream of celery soup
1 bag, 12 oz. of egg noodles
Olive oil
Salt/pepper

Saute garlic in 2 - 3 tablespoons of olive oil with your Dutch sitting over 10 - 12 briquets. Brown the chicken, then add the onions, three cans of beer, and the soup. Arrange 14 - 16 briquets around the outside of the lid and cook for 1 - 2 hours. If your birds are old, plan on having a little more charcoal to add in order to cook them longer. After about 2 hours remove the charcoal from the lid and take the lid off the Dutch. Add the last can of beer, or whatever you're using for cooking liquid, to just cover the pieces of chicken. Add the egg noodles and stir them enough so they're covered with liquid. Place Dutch back in the fire pan over 12 - 14 briquets for 20 - 30 minutes, but do not put any charcoal on the lid. Let set 10 - 15 minutes before serving.

Serves 4 to 6

BUTCH'S BITCHIN' CHICKEN

Ingredients:

6 - 8 boneless/skinned chicken breasts
1 ½ cups white cooking wine or chicken stock
½ cup oil-pack dried tomatoes, diced up
½ cup pine nuts
4 oz. dried spinach fettucine
4 oz. dried fettucinee
½ cup pesto
Salt/pepper/Italian Seasoning

Season chicken breasts and arrange in 12" Dutch. Pour in the cooking liquid. Set the Dutch on a firepan with 10 - 14 briquets underneath and let simmer for 30 - 40 minutes.

Prepare fettucine according to package directions. Drain and dress with pesto then spoon over the chicken breasts in the Dutch.

Sprinkle the top with dried tomatoes and pine nuts and let simmer over the charcoal another 15 minutes.

Serves 6

Often times for river trips I'll grill the breasts at home and freeze them which alleviates the worry of them spoiling.

Words of Wisdom

On long trips when salad fixin's won't keep long enough, plan a five or seven bean salad. A pasta salad also will add some variety.

BECK'S HONEY MUSTARD
—————— ROASTED CHICKEN ——————

My pard, ex-roommate from college days, river running nut, Tom Beck provided this quick and tasty recipe. While your chicken is roasting in a 12" DO, get a pot of rice going in your 10" DO for a quick two pot supper. Tom, aka "Catfish", first used honey mustard for this dish, but you can substitute barbeque sauce, sweet and sour sauce, or something similiar to suit yourself.

Ingredients:

1 frying chicken cut into pieces
¾ cup water or white wine
½ cup prepared honey mustard
Salt/pepper or other seasonings to taste

"Catfish" uses a circular, wire rack which just fits in the bottom of a 12" Dutch. He found his at a yard sale. If you can't find something similar, you can use several rings from canning jars placed in the Dutch. Brush the honey mustard on the chicken and let set for a few minutes while the charcoal gets going. Put your rack in the bottom of the Dutch and add the water and or wine. Arrange the chicken pieces skin side up on the rack and season with salt and pepper. (I like to use something along the lines of Mrs. Dash® which adds a little color as well.) Set the Dutch in your firepan with 4 - 5 briquets going underneath. Line the outside of the lid with 18 - 22 briquets with three or four over the center of the lid. Roast for about forty-five minutes to an hour. If you want, set your 10" Dutch on top of your 12" Dutch and let the the charcoal cook in two directions.
Serves 4 - 6

Tom Beck

STUFFED CORNISH GAME HENS

Ingredients:

5 Cornish game hens 16 - 21 oz. each
5 small, mild onions
5 packages, 4 oz. each of wild rice with herbs
2 cups dry white wine or chicken stock
2 -3 cloves of garlic sliced/diced
Olive oil
Whole cloves
Salt/pepper + your favorite seasonings

Prepare game hens by washing and then dusting the body cavity with seasonings. Rub birds with enough olive oil to make them glisten. Stuff each game hen with a small onion with two or three whole cloves stuck in it.

Prepare the rice and herb mix according to package directions but reduce the liquid by $1/_3$ and cooking time by ½. Set birds aside and saute the garlic in 3 - 4 tablespoons of olive oil. When garlic turns golden brown, gently fry each bird for 2 - 3 minutes. Then arrange the birds in a 14" Dutch and add wine or chicken stock. Put 2 - 3 tablespoons of rice in each bird. Spoon remaining rice around the birds. Dust the top of the birds with your seasonings.

Cook for about an hour with 8 - 10 briquets underneath and 15 or so briquets arranged around the outside flange of the lid.

To vary this recipe try different rice/seasoning mixes.

To give this a fancy touch, pull the lid about 10 minutes before serving and garnish with broccoli florets. If you want to make a "one pot" dinner out of this, place 5 - 4 medium carrots cut in 1" pieces in about half an hour after starting and the broccoli ten minutes before dinner.

BLUE GROUSE CACCIATORE
———— (CHUKARS, PHEASANT) ————

Ingredients:

2 blue grouse, cut in serving pieces
2 - 3 Tbsp. olive oil
2 - 3 cloves of garlic, peeled and pressed

Saute pressed garlic in olive oil 2-3 minutes until brown.
Lightly brown birds in olive oil.

Mix:

2 large cans tomato paste
2 large cans tomato sauce
1 Tbsp. Italian seasoning
2 medium cans stewed tomatoes

While birds are frying, mix tomato paste and tomato sauce
together in bowl along with 1 Tbsp. Italian seasoning.
When birds are lightly browned, transfer them to large
casserole dish or Dutch oven. Pour mixture of tomato
sauce and tomato paste over them. Then add stewed
tomatoes.

Add:

2 small onions, diced
1 can olives, sliced
2 small cans mushrooms, sliced

Place vegetables over the top and sprinkle additional Italian
seasoning over the top.

Bake at 350 - 375 degrees for 1 hour. Serve over rice.

Serves 4.

_____ SARA'S CAMP CHICKEN _____

This recipe is so easy, even a pilgrim can put it together and make a meal fit for a King — at camp or at home in the backyard.

It can be cooked in most any standard casserole dish, pan or Dutch. We just happen to prefer cast iron Dutches and chicken cookers.

Ingredients:

6 chicken breasts (boneless and skinless)
1 package Lipton® Onion soup mix
1 jar, 8 oz. apricot jam
1 bottle, 8 oz. Catalina (or Russian) salad dressing

Brown chicken in cast iron pan. Mix other ingredients and pour over the chicken. Cook for at least one hour. Sauce should be thick.

Serve with steamed or wild rice.

Note: You can use other chicken parts or even a whole chicken - just be sure the chicken is well done.

Sara Brown, aka Grandma Brown
Twin Falls, ID

_____Words of Wisdom _____

In the summer, at least part of your main dish meats may be pre-cooked to extend their life in a camp cooler, i.e. chicken breasts, ham steaks, sausage links can be pre-cooked and then frozen.

STREAM-SIDE SALMON

Ingredients:

Aluminum foil
1 Salmon fillet, 2-3 lbs.
Salt and pepper, lemon pepper works, too!
½ cup sour cream
1 onion, sliced into rings
1 lemon, sliced into rings
Fresh dill or dried dill weed

Arrange aluminum foil to be double wrapped and have a closed seam for cooking. Lay the Salmon fillet on the tin foil. Dust the fillet with salt and pepper. Lemon pepper works well, too. Sprinkle fresh dill or dried dill on the fillet. Brush sour cream on the fillet abundantly. Place thin slices of onion and lemon over the fillet. Wrap up the fillet in the tin foil. Place directly over briquets or on the coals of your campfire on a low fire. Turn fillet over after about 20 minutes and cook for approximately 20 more minutes. Depending on how hot your coals are, cooking time can be reduced to 15 minutes per side.

—Aside—For those who don't like fish, here's another easy tin foil entree to cook along with your fish dinner.

SCOUT BURGER

Ingredients:

Aluminum foil
Several pads of butter, or equivalent
½ - 1 lb of hamburger, formed into a patty
1-2 potatoes, diced
1 onion, diced
2 carrots, sliced
Salt and pepper

Make a tray of aluminum foil. Put the butter on the foil. Place the hamburger on top of the butter. Place the vegetables on top of the hamburger and add the seasoning. Wrap up the contents in the foil and cook by placing in coals of a campfire or firepan. Place a few hot coals on top.

___ CAMPFIRE POACHED FISH ___

Fill a large frying pan at least 1½ inches deep with water, broth, dry white wine, or a combination. Add 2 teaspoons mixed pickling spice, sprigs of mint, if available, or your favorite spices. Onion, carrot, or celery stalk pieces are other possible seasonings. Add salt and pepper to taste. Slip cleaned and scaled fish into liquid and simmer gently, uncovered, until fish flakes when poked with a fork. Drain and serve.

The Hollandaise sauce below is really good with this dish.

Cathy Robertson
Twin Falls, ID

EASY FRYING PAN HOLLANDAISE

Melt in a small frying pan over a low fire, 1 tablespoon butter cut from a ¼ pound cube; remove from heat. separate 2 eggs (save or discard whites) and stir yolks and 1 teaspoon Dijon-style mustard smoothly into butter. On the prongs of a fork, spear remaining 7 tablespoons firm butter amd replace pan over low fire. Vigorously stir butter as it slowly melts, blending thouroughly thorughout egg mixture until sauce thickens slightly. Remove pan from heat; stir in about 1 tablespoon lemon juice. Makes about 1 cup.

Cathy Robertson
Twin Falls, ID

SEVICHE

Ingredients:

6 cups chopped fish
Lemon Juice

Cover fish with lemon juice and refrigerate over night in glass or ceramic dish. Do not use metal dishes.

3 cups chopped tomatoes
3 cups chopped onions
1 cup diced green chilies
15 diced green olives
4 Tbsp. Worcestershire sauce
1½ Tbsp. salt
4 cloves garlic, chopped
2 tsp. Tabasco® sauce
2 tsp. olive oil
3 tsp. catsup

Mix in remaining ingredients. Cover and marinate at least four more hours. Serve with crackers.

Stacy Gebhards
Region 3 Supervisor, Boise
Idaho Department of Fish and Game

Words of Wisdom

For a fresh-caught flavor, thaw fish in milk.

Lemons don't take much room and keep fairly well so throw a few of them in your chuck box. Bottled lemon juice will work as well. Besides using them for cooking, squeeze the juice of a lemon over meat or chicken prior to cooking to eliminate that "ice box" taste.

HOW to COOK a COOT

If you're not a duck hunter or married to a duck hunter, just skip this recipe. Personally, I've never tried to cook a coot, primarily because I've never even shot at an "Ivory Billed Mallard". Remember, this is the guy who will eat every thing except grits and green lima beans.

In this modern age, it seems to me, too many people blame events in their childhood for the mistakes or failures they make as adults. Some rightly so, but I can't help but feel a lot of it is over done!

So where is all this leading, you ask yourself? Yup! you guessed it, my childhood. Since my dad first took me duck hunting at age three, the list of things I've done in life longer than I've duck hunted is fairly short.

Memories of those first duck hunts are still vivid. Back in that distant past, I learned that the preferred duck of those who wait at home while others duck hunt, to be mallards. Those of the green headed variety!

My dad, being a pretty fair hand with a shotgun, seldom got skunked in those days. He'd been there before, but it was a new experience for me, just four years old. About the only thing flying in the marsh that day were coots, which Dad had several different adjectives to describe. I didn't understand why dad didn't shoot them as they patterned by. At that time I obviously thought–ducks are ducks! Wrong!

How long I pestered Dad to shoot them, I can't remember. What I do remember is him saying, "Mother didn't like any kind of ducks except those with green heads" and it wouldn't be very smart to take something home she didn't like. Though I was just four years old, that part I understood!

I'm sure Dad first passed this recipe on that day. Over the years, Dad repeated this recipe so many times I've memorized it without ever having cooked it.

ROAST COOT by BUZZ

Dress out as many coots as you can find folks (fools) who will accept an invitation for a coot dinner. i.e. allow one coot per fool or one fool per coot! Birds should be dressed out within one month of being shot.

Soak birds for 2 - 3 days in salt water. (Use 2 - 3 lbs. salt per gallon of water)

Rinse birds and pat dry. Place each bird on a cedar shingle which you've seasoned to taste.

Place coots and shingles in a preheated oven, 450 - 500 degrees for eight hours. (Smoke usually clears out in 3 - 4 hrs.)

Allow to cool about thirty minutes. Scrape the coots off of the shingles into a steel drum for transport to a "Hazardous Materials Disposal Center."

Serve shingles garnished with crab apples!

Camp Chili, Stews, Soups & Sauces

CHILI
THE CONTROVERSY
THE RECIPES
&
A BACK COUNTRY LEARNING
EXPERIENCE!

Up until the time I became friends with a bunch of Texans in the mid 1970's, I had no idea chili didn't have beans in it. I grew up thinking chili consisted of beans, venison burger, onions, tomato sauce and some Mexican seasoning simmered in a pot and served with canned tamales. Little did I know in some regions of the country, one stood the chance of a camp court martial for putting beans in the chili*#! Only in person, could you truly appreciate the sarcastic oaths aimed in my direction by three Texans, just in from a hard day chasing elk, when they found beans in their chili. Let me explain.

The fall of 1977, while working for the Inter-Agency Grizzly Bear Study, I and another fellow were dispatched to try to trap a grizzly bothering an outfitter camp just east of Yellowstone Park. The boss warned us we might get a cool reception from the outfitter, since this bear had already torn up a couple of tents and other gear. A forest service packer would pack us and our gear in and drop us off near the camp for a ten day hitch. Dave and I worried for the thirteen mile ride up Fishhawk Creek about having to camp next to a group of belligerent hunters for ten days.

It was not uncommon, even then, for folks to consider capital punishment equitable treatment for any bear tearing up a hunting camp. Our orders were to trap the bear, put a radio collar on it, and hike back to our truck without getting embroiled in any confrontations! The outfitter, who turned out to be a transplanted Texan, along with his brother in-law and another friend, greeted us as soon as we pulled into their camp.

To this day, after almost eighteen years as a game warden, I've never received a friendlier greeting than we did that day! (More often than not, about 50% of the time, we're greeted like a carrier of a socially communicable disease!) Since the boss planned on us hiking out, we arrived with a little back pack tent and ten days' worth of freeze dried food.

Fred, Howard and Kirk insisted on putting up another wall tent with a stove for us to stay in, saying it would bother their conscience to even think of us shivering each morning in that flimsy little tent! While stowing our gear in the newly erected wall tent, Howard asked us if the packer had forgot to unload our food. "No," Dave said as he pulled a plastic garbage sack out of his back pack and showed them our freeze dried food. Once again these big hearted Texans intervened. Fred said we could use it to supplement the "dawgs food" if we wanted to, but he wouldn't hear of people eating such "#?*&" while they stayed in his camp.

At dinner that evening in Fred's big cook tent, we feasted on T-Bone steak, all the trimmin's and washed it down with branch water and good Southern sippin' whiskey! Look up "hospitality" in the dictionary and you should see a picture of three Texas hunters sitting in a wall tent with gas lanterns illuminating their smilin' faces. About the time Kirk went to fetch more branch water from the crick, Fred asked if they took the next day off from hunting, could they help us make our bear sets?

Dave and I went to bed that night thinking we'd cut a purty fat hog in the butt! The next day the five of us spent until early afternoon building cubbies where Dave and I set our Aldrich Bear Snares. To show our gratitude, Dave and I teamed up with a cross cut saw and spent the rest of the day reducing a nearby blow down tree to firewood. The next morning, just as the stars began to dim, I heard a awful caterwauling just up the meadow from camp. My first thought was we'd caught our bear the very first night. As I shook off the cobwebs, I recognized the source of the noise as "Bumper", Fred's magnum size Black Lab! By the time I managed to release Bumper without getting bit, Fred had a lantern going in the cook tent. By this time everyone in camp was up and getting dressed. After having a laugh at Bumper's expense, Howard cooked breakfast while Dave and I helped Fred saddle horses. They headed out of camp in the grey light of dawn leaving Dave and me to check our sets. By 0830 we were back in camp sipping coffee.

Without a bear in a snare, a bear trapper normally ends up with lots of time on his hands. With two days down and eight to go, Dave and I began a routine of doing the camp chores. In addition, I took over the cooking duties so Fred didn't have to worry it when he came in from hunting each night.

Both Dave and I, being from SE Idaho, were experiencing Texans and their culture, first hand, for the first time! Within a day or two we were both answering to "Yankee". By day five the only faux paux either of us had committed was one morning when Dave insisted on putting ketchup on his eggs instead of salsa. Things were going good except the bear we'd been sent to trap had hauled freight out of the country. Other than that, we'd comfortably settled into the routine of camp.

Day six (just another day, or so I thought) dawned with a cold wind blowing out of the north and slate grey clouds scudding from ridge to ridge. It just seemed like a "chili day" to Dave and me. Refer to the first paragraph of this story for the chili recipe I used that day. Dave kept the wood stove cranking out heat, while I started a pot of what later became known as blankety, blankety, blank, blank **"YANKEE CHILI"!**

Actually everything went pretty well for everyone that day, up until I started to serve supper. Fred, Howard, and Kirk came in just at dark as Mother Nature started to spit snow with a vengeance. Fred said he could smell the chili three hundred yards downwind as he plopped the liver of a five point bull into a tin basin. Howard poured five shots of internal fire starter as Fred told Dave and I about getting the bull. Kirk came in from the sleeping tent and asked what was for dinner, as he shook the snow off his coat and grabbed a shot of fire starter.

Wiping my hands on the commandeered apron, I replied the chili, flour tortillas, along with extra cheese and onions only needed another twenty minutes or so. Dave set the table while Fred and Howard headed out to grain the horses. I could see fifty cent size snowflakes falling outside when they pulled the tent flap back to come in for supper. I won't say anticipation was running at fever pitch but it is safe to say everyone was looking foward to eating someone else's cooking that night! "Going to hell in a hand basket", aptly describes the out cry when I served Howard the first bowl of chili.

In less time than it took to write this paragraph, I learned the difference between "real Texas Chili" and "Yankee Chili"! All three Texans, who I'd thought to be BIG hearted and hospitable, turned on me like General Sam Houston turned on General Santa Anna at the battle of San Jacinto! No mercy was shown this "Yankee" from Idaho. "Only a Yankee would put beans in chili," Howard roared! In a not so nice tone of voice, (forgetting momentarily whose tent I slept in and whose food I'd been eating for a week) I asked just what the hell his definition of a "Yankee" was? Matching my sarcasm, Howard replied, anyone from north of San Antonio! I obviously fit the definition. Howard informed me if you want beans with your chili in Texas, they're served as a side dish!

Rather than repeat the verbal abuse or have the editors delete all the expletives, I'll just include some recipes from both north and south of San Antonio. For a short, comprehensive history, loaded with great chili recipes, get ahold of a copy of the **CHILI LOVERS' COOK BOOK** by Al Fischer and Mildred Fischer which is published by Golden West publishers of Phoenix, Arizona.

HOWARD'S
SOUTH TEXAS CHILI

Ingredients:

2 lbs. flank steak cut in 1" pieces
2 large onions diced
6 cloves of garlic minced or sliced thin
1 cup tomato sauce
1 cup tomato juice
1 cup tomato paste
1 cup of water
1 tsp. salt
½ tsp. black pepper (coarse grind)
½ tsp. cayenne pepper
¾ tsp. cumin
¾ tsp. oregano
½ cup dark chili powder
4 - 5 Tbsp. flour
Olive oil

Set a 14" DO in the firepan with 12 - 16 briquets underneath. Add 3 - 4 Tbsp. olive oil and saute the garlic for about 3 - 4 minutes. Put the meat in and fry with the salt, pepper and onions for about ten minutes before you add the tomato juice, sauce, paste, and water. Allow to simmer for 10 - 15 minutes. Mix the dry spices with the flour and stir into the meat. Cook for another 1½ - 2 hours. Decrease cooking time a little if you use ground meat instead of flank steak. The flour will thicken the chili as it cooks. Add a little water if you like it thinner.

Serves and keeps warm 8 - 10 hungry hunters

Howard Konetzke, Jr.
LaGrange, Texas

CEE DUB'S YANKEE CHILI

Ingredients:

1 lb. dry pinto, Anasazi, or kidney beans
2 lbs. ground venison or burger (I prefer a coarse grind for burger)
2 large onions cut in chunks
1 can, 28 oz. of stewed tomatoes
1 can, 28 oz. of tomato sauce
2 cups of water
6 cloves of garlic, sliced thin
3 Tbsp. store-bought Mexican seasoning
1 tsp. garlic powder
½ cup chili powder
½ tsp. salt
½ tsp. coarse ground pepper
Olive oil

The night before, put your beans to soak in a large stock pot with enough water to cover them with 4 - 5 inches of water. The next day, when you come back to camp for lunch, drain and rinse the beans.

Set a 14" DO over 10 - 15 briquets and pour in the beans with the tomato sauce and stewed tomatoes. Add the dry spices and onions as well. Let this start to simmer while you saute the garlic in 2 - 3 Tbsp. of olive oil in another DO or frying pan. After the garlic turns a golden color add the meat and continue to fry for 10 - 15 minutes. Drain any excess grease off and add to the Dutch with the beans. Simmer for 1- 2 hours or until everyone gets in off the hill.

Serves about 6 hunters

If you have any leftover chili, reheat it and serve with eggs and warmed tortillas and salsa for breakfast the next morning.

HOWARD'S ONION,
— CHILI & CHEESE CASSEROLE —

Hunting camps are the home of many different traditions. Rather than name them all, by now you should've figured out, eating good in camp is one of the more important traditions in my camp. If what I hear from others is true, most folks do indeed look foward each year, not only to the hunt, but to the eating as well!

A friend of mine, Howard Konetzke, Jr., of LaGrange, Texas, serves this for lunch or dinner when he and his crew go whitetail hunting out in south Texas. Howard guarantees if you make it with his chili recipe, it will keep everyone in camp warm and going!

Ingredients:

½ Batch of Texas style chili (see page 141)
4 large yellow onions, sliced
2 lbs. of Velveeta cheese sliced as thin as you can
3 dozen corn tortillas, cut in 1½" strips

Take a 14" DO and spoon some of the chili into the bottom of the Dutch. About ½" will do. Take your tortilla strips and cover the chili with your strips all running the same direction. Next, add another layer of tortilla strips running at right angles to the first layer. Now, place a layer of onion slices over the chili then add a layer of cheese slices.

Repeat the process till you've used all the onion slices and velveeta cheese. Bake in the Dutch for about 30 - 40 minutes with 14 - 16 briquets underneath and about an equal number on top. Howard says don't be stingy with the onions!

Serves 8-10

CHILI CON CARNE with BEANS

Ingredients:

2 lbs. elk or beef flank steak cut in 1" chunks
1 ½ lbs. dry pinto/small red kidney beans
2 large onions
1 can, 29 oz. tomato sauce
1 can, 16 oz. stewed tomatoes
1 can, 4 oz. diced green chilies (jalapenos, if you
     like it hot)
6 - 8 cloves of garlic, thinly sliced
¼ cup olive oil
2 Tbsp. chili powder
4 Tbsp. Mexican seasoning
Salt and pepper
Water

The night before you plan to have a chili feed, rinse the beans and let them soak over night with twice the amount of water as beans. The next morning, drain the beans and put them in a deep 14" DO with enough water to cover them, then set the DO over 12 - 16 briquets in a firepan. This takes a fair amount of time to cook, so have extra charcoal handy. (Or set the DO on your gas or propane camp stove on as low a setting as possible.) Let them simmer for a couple of hours, adding

charcoal to the firepan as needed. I always add about half of my seasoning and diced onions when I put the chili on to simmer.

After the beans have simmered for a couple of hours, saute the garlic in another DO until golden brown over 6 - 8 briquets. Add another 6 - 8 briquets and brown the meat over this higher heat. While the meat is browning put the tomato sauce, chilies and stewed tomatoes in the DO with the beans. Add the remainder of your spices to the browning meat and stir to mix. When the meat has browned for about ten minutes spoon the meat over to the other DO. Continue to simmer for another hour or two. While this is cooking mix up a batch of corn bread to make for a bunch of happy campers.

Note: I soak my beans in a kettle or stock pot and not in an iron Dutch.

Serves 10 - 12

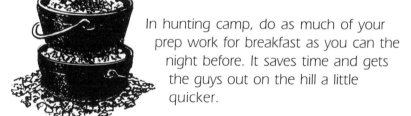

_____ Words of Wisdom _____

In hunting camp, do as much of your prep work for breakfast as you can the night before. It saves time and gets the guys out on the hill a little quicker.

Whether car camping, horse packing or on a raft trip, organize your camp boxes and cooler. That way, in the grey light of dawn, while every one is straining at the bit to get going, you're not going through all five coolers to find the sausage.

Some dishes, such as soups, stews, chili with beans, and casseroles, can be made at home and frozen. These are extra nice in hunting camp when the first guy back to camp can start it heating, so when every one else gets in supper is done with little muss or fuss.

BRUNEAU RIVER
GREEN PORK CHILI & ENCHILADAS

I first made this a few years ago for an April float trip down the Bruneau River in Owyhee County, Idaho. In order to save time in camp I made this up at home ahead of time. In that case it turned out to be a real time saver, as the "River Gods" provided a four hour rain shower about the time we stopped for the day. I recommend you fix this, like I did, ahead of time or on a day you plan to spend in camp.

Ingredients: Green Pork Chili

1   3 - 4 lb. pork roast
2   Tbsp. cumin
3   Tbsp. corn starch
6   cups water
1   4 oz. can green chilies drained and finely diced
      or, fresh green, anaheim and jalapeno peppers, minced
1 lb. tomatillas, minced
Salt and pepper
½ tsp. each of dried minced onion and garlic.

After you get the charcoal started, wash your hands and rub the cumin on the roast. Salt and pepper the roast at this time if you wish. This works best in a deep 12" DO, if you have one. Place the roast in the DO with a couple of cups of water, of course, minced fresh garlic may be added, too, as garlic goes with just about everything except strawberry short cake! Set the DO in the fire pan with 12 - 14 briquets both underneath and on the lid. Roast slowly for 3 - 4 hours, adding charcoal every 1½ hours. Check occasionally and add water to keep about an inch of liquid in the Dutch. When the roast will just fall apart, it's done. Pull the roast out and set it aside to cool. Pull your DO off the fire and cover with the lid until the roast has cooled. Once the roast is cool to the touch, trim off any fat and shred or chop coarsely with a knife. Set the DO you did the roast in over 6 - 8 fresh briquets and add ¼ of your shredded meat along with four cups water, the chilies, or peppers and tomatillas and the minced onion and garlic. Stir to mix and let this simmer for 15 - 20 minutes. A tablespoon at a time, mix the cornstarch with cold water and stir into the meat until it thickens to suit you. Presto, you've just made green pork chili ! If you make this at home and want to use it later, let it cool and refrigerate in a couple of old plastic butter tubs.

Ingredients: Pork Enchiladas

1 dozen burrito size flour tortillas
2 cups grated cheddar
      and/or monterey jack cheese
1 can of black olives drained and diced
1 small yellow onion diced
1 container of fresh salsa
1 cup of green pork chili

Set a 12" DO over 6 - 8 evenly spaced briquets and let heat for about 10 minutes. One at a time take a tortilla and let warm for 10 - 15 seconds at a time then flip over for another 10 - 15 seconds.

Take each warmed "tort" and place 2 - 3 tablespoons of shredded pork, a tablespoon of green pork chili, 1 teaspoon of salsa, along with a teaspoon each of diced onion and olive on each tortilla. Roll up and place in a 12" DO with a thin layer of green pork chili spread on the bottom. Since you can only fit about six enchiladas in a 12" DO you'll need a couple of Dutches or in a pinch put two layers in one 12" DO. Pour the remaining green pork chili over the enchiladas and bake with 16 - 18 briquets on the top and 4 - 6 on the bottom for 30 - 40 minutes.

Take the DO off the firepan and spread the grated cheese over the top and let set for 10 minutes before you serve. It shouldn't take a rocket scientist to figure out you can make this with chicken, beef, or whatever you have in the cooler.

STEW

My pocket dictionary defines stew as "to boil slowly" or "a dish of stewed meat and vegetables served in gravy". So even for those folks whose cooking talents are stretched by just trying to boil water, they only have to add some meat and veggies to make a stew. In other words, beginning Dutch oven cooks and stews were made for each other. Someone with a new Dutch oven, wanting to cook something, is just like a student pilot landing an airplane. Any landing you walk away from is good, some are just better than others! For first time Dutch oven cooks, that translates to if your dinner guests do not leave the supper table in search of immediate medical attention, it must've been okay! As with flying and many other things for that matter, the results usually improve with a little practice.

You can make a stew as simple as Tony Latham's "Warden Stew" or create a masterpiece containing exotic vegetables and spices. If you're bored with just plain old cooking and you want to try "ethnic cooking" there is no better place to start than with a stew. For example, take your Great-great-great Grandmother's stew recipe which she brought West in a covered wagon and add some oriental vegetables and seasoning to create a stew with a distinctive, new taste.

Most of us who hunt big game, when rummaging around our freezers, leave those packages of meat labeled "stew" until everything else has been used. At least the way I cut up my animals, the amount of stew meat always exceeds what I'd call prime cuts.

Though you can't cut chunks of elk shank with a fork when fried in butter, to me it's no reason to leave it till last. Cooked slow in a Dutch oven with your favorite veggies and spices, an old elk shank will produce as many oh's and ah's as tenderloin sauteed in butter and garlic! A good mathematician could fill a fair sized room with nothing but stew recipes by calculating all the combinations and permutations of possible ingredients for stew. So if you fancy your self a creative person, take your new Dutch oven and a "Stew" recipe and create a master piece!

Around my house or camp, stew tends to end up as a "kitchen sink" dish. i.e. everything except the kitchen sink is likely to be thrown in the pot. As a result no two are the same. Besides being easy to make, nothing tastes better when one comes in from the cold than a steaming bowl of stew and a chunk of homemade bread.

On more than one occasion the last night in camp, dinner consisted of some leftover meat and everything else left in the bottom of the camp box with some baking powder biscuits to soak up the juices. What ever the occasion, whether at home or in camp, A Dutch oven stew will fill'em up and keep'em smilin'

_____ GOSPEL HUMP SOUP _____

Ingredients:

1 can of chicken soup
Left over pasta
1 can kidney beans
Summer squash or zucchini
2-4 tomatoes
Other leftovers that might be in the camp box or kitchen

Put all ingredients into a Dutch oven and simmer for a few minutes to blend the flavors. Serve with bread or salad for a complete meal in a jiffy.

CAMP CROCK POT

A few years ago in September, I'd horse packed into Bear Valley, Idaho to check archery hunters. I broke camp and pulled out fairly early in the morning. Over a half mile out from the trailhead I could hear a motor running. When I got there I found a big camp had been set up next to where I'd parked my truck and trailer. By the time I'd unpacked and grained the stock this generator was beginning to get on my nerves.

The best description I can give of this camp would be to call it an "aluminum wagon train". There were three travel trailers of varying sizes and two pickups with large cabover campers all parked in a circle. All five "wagons" were connected by extension cords of different lengths to a trailer mounted generator. When I walked up everyone was sitting around in the September sunshine swapping stories and sipping drinks which clinked with ice cubes. Setting on a camp table were two large crock pots which the camp cook told me contained the only game they'd gotten. Dinner, he said, was going to be "Blue Grouse Fricassee". He continued by saying, it sure was nice to come back to camp after the evening hunt and have dinner ready to go.

Now I can't argue with that, but I prefer camping in a place which doesn't sound so much like a construction site! Don't get me wrong, because I like some of today's amenities in camp, but running a generator of that size just to power a couple of crock pots falls into the "overkill" category. Not only did I have to raise my voice somewhat to be heard, but every other camp within a half mile had to put up with the noise as well.

Other than battery power in my flashlight, the closest I've been to having an all electric camp was the time I pitched camp along side a currant bush thicket. These bushes didn't produce any voltage but the "juice" produced from a couple of cups of berries, with a little sugar added, made for some awful good french toast. But.... read on if you'd like the convenience of a crock pot without the aggravation of having to listen to a generator all afternoon.

When you set up camp, dig a hole about two feet deep right next to where you put your campfire. (Keep the dirt in a pile close by cause you're going to need it later.) This hole should be about twice the size of your Dutch oven. That night while you fix supper, start a fire in your hole and let it burn down before you hit the bed ground. Next morning as soon as you get the coffee going, start both fires and pile on a fair amount of wood.

While you're cooking breakfast, get the number two cook to put all the makins' of a stew or a pot roast in a Dutch. Make sure he seasons it and adds a little more cooking liquid than usual. Put the lid on and spin it around just to make sure it doesn't have a gap from being on crooked. Take a couple of feet of baling wire and wrap one end on the bail of the Dutch oven. (Make sure you don't use the handle on the lid.)

About the time breakfast is over both fires should have burned back to coals. With your camp shovel, scoop a small depression in the coals in the hole. Set your Dutch oven in the depression and shovel the coals from your camp fire onto the Dutch until it's covered. Now shovel all the dirt you saved when you dug the hole over the coals on top of the Dutch oven. You should have 6" - 8" of dirt over top the coals. If you did it right, the wire tied to the bail should indicate where the Dutch oven is. Douse any left over coals in your campfire, so when you leave there are no live coals left to be a fire danger.

That evening when you get to camp, dinner will be piping hot and ready to serve. Carefully shovel off the dirt and coals until you're down to the lid of the Dutch oven. Using the wire you wrapped on the bail gently lift the Dutch out and set it down. I keep an old whisk broom in my camp box to brush the remaining dirt and coals off the lid. (Most folks will appreciate the meal better without a shovel full of grit added just prior to serving!) Anyway...there you have it, a "camp crock pot" with out having to pack around a generator and an extension cord.

WINTER'S DAY STEW

Ingredients:

Saute together:
1 ½ to 2 lbs. venison steak or roast cut into 1" pieces
2 Tbsp. olive oil
2 cups diced onions
2 cloves garlic, minced

Transfer to 2 quart (or larger) crock pot or Dutch oven.

Add:
2 Tbsp. flour
1 tsp. Cinnamon
1 tsp. ground cumin
¾ cup cider
¾ cup dark beer
4 cups diced winter squash (acorn or banana are best)
Salt and pepper to taste
1 cup chopped green peppers
2 cups chopped apples

Slow cook 5 - 6 hours on low or until tender.

Phillis Kochert
Office Coordinator, Administration
Idaho Department of Fish and Game, Boise

BASIC VENISON STEW

Ingredients:

2 lbs. elk stew meat cut in 1" to 2" cubes*
2 lbs. potatoes cut in chunks
2 lbs. carrots cut in 1" pieces
6 - 8 stalks of celery cut in 1" pieces
1 - 2 Tbsp. flour**
2 - 3 onions cut in wedges
4 - 5 cloves of garlic, minced
Olive oil
Salt and Pepper/seasonings
4 - 5 bay leaves
4 - 5 cups of water

Saute the garlic in a little olive oil until golden brown. While browning the garlic, dredge the meat in the flour. Brown the meat for about ten minutes. Add the water and bay leaves and then set the DO in the firepan with 8 - 10 briquets underneath and allow to simmer for 40 - 50 minutes. At this point add your vegetables and check the amount of liquid in the Dutch. Put additional briquets in the firepan and cook another 45 minutes or until veggies are done.

* Use the cooking times given for good cuts of stew meat. If you're using shank meat with a lot of gristle at least double the length of time you simmer the meat before adding the vegetables.
** The flour used to dredge the meat will naturally thicken your stew. To have more of a broth and less of a gravy like liquid, just brown your meat without dredging it in flour.

WARDEN STEW

This camp cookbook tends to focus on "sagebrush gourmet", or in more civilized circles what's referred to as fancy cookin'! Yet, there comes a time when it's "hold the garnish, hold the special herbs, hold the time spent slicing and dicing, and hold digging through all the horse packs for a measuring spoon, let's just get something on the fire so we can eat and hit the sack"! Tony Latham, an Idaho Game Warden, aka the "Laser" who has spent more time kicking around the Central Idaho wilderness areas than most, wanted to pass on his favorite "Wilderness Fast Food" recipe.

To those outside the wildlife law enforcement fraternity, let me preface this recipe with a little of my own experience. Here in Idaho, the typical game warden has in excess of a thousand square miles to patrol. Obviously, some patrol areas are larger than others, with back country patrol areas up to three times the average. During the fall big game seasons, it's an understatement to say one can get spread "purty thin" tryin' to effectively patrol areas of such size!

It reminded me of an old warden buddy of mine, who used to tell of trying to feed a whole troop of boy scouts with two little dinky hatchery trout and a bag of stale hamburger buns! Kinda tough to get enough to go around without divine intervention.

It doesn't matter if you're jerking a string of horses in the back country, trying to float an extra mile before darkness sets in, pulling one's truck off on an old log road at midnite, or getting home in the wee hours, "Lasers Warden Stew" sure beats the hell out of dreaming about over priced, foreign sounding dishes at restaurants four hours by plane away!

LASER'S WARDEN STEW

Ingredients:

1   package elk burger
Some red potatoes, cut "the quicker you want to
    eat, the smaller you cut them."
Some onions, cut them just like the taters.
Some pepper
Some garlic powder or minced garlic
Some slices of Swiss Cheese
Some cooking liquid (Water will do, one or two
    beers is even better, and Laser says that dark beer
    makes it best.)

Get a fire and/or coals going as soon as you can. Dump everything but the cheese slices in a 12" DO and cook until the liquid has reduced by ½ - ¾. Take the lid off and place the cheese slices over the top. Let cook for a few minutes, or until you can't take it any longer, then serve. Reheat the left overs while you make coffee in the morning and "voila" you've just experienced "Wilderness Fast Food" times two!

Laser will agree his isn't a prize winnin' recipe, but under field conditions it will get you there and back!

Words of Wisdom

When you pull camp make an extra trip around the camp site after you're all packed. Pick up any stray snoose cans or gum wrappers. It's also insurance against leaving a fishing rod leaning up against a tree.

When packing garbage crush all your cans and plastic bottles. If possible "toast" your cans for a few minutes in the camp fire to burn off food residues.

____ STEFFADO (RABBIT STEW) ____

Ingredients:

1 rabbit (or chicken)
½ cup olive oil
½ cup vinegar
1 can tomatoes
1 cup beer (omit if spinach is used)
2 medium onions
Herbs (oregano, bay leaf, cloves, etc.)
1 cup garlic (yes! a cup, or more)
4 bunches spinach (2 cans or 1 bag frozen)

Combine all ingredients together, EXCEPT spinach, in a Dutch oven and boil for one to three hours. Remove bones, add spinach, and cook until tender. Add more beer if additional liquid is needed. Serve with lemon slices, French bread and Parmesan cheese.

Serves 4

Shelley and Don Anderson
Region 3 Fisher Manager, McCall, Idaho
Idaho Department Fish & Game

____ Words of Wisdom ____

Always pack the **EXTRAS.** The extra mantles for the lanterns, the extra batteries for the flashlight, extra whiskey or beverage of choice for the cook, extra **TP** in case someone gets into some bad water, extra matches in case some one leaves them out in the rain, and any other little extras you need in camp.

BASIC SOUP STOCK

Thumb though a couple of your cook books and I'm sure you'll notice recipes which call for beef stock or chicken stock. Most of these recipes will also mention that bouillon cubes may be used as a substitute. Any kind of stock is easily made either at home or in camp. I prefer to use the home made variety myself, just because I believe it is a little healthier. Check the label on the store bought varieties and you'll find salt is always one of the primary ingredients. Make your own and you'll end up with better flavor and less salt. When I butcher a deer or elk, I set some bones aside to make a couple of batches of soup stock to freeze. I find neck and hock bones make the best stock just because the longer legs bones require too large of a pot.

Ingredients:

4 - 5 lbs. of bones with some meat still on the
    bone
1 - 2 gals. of water
1 large onion diced up
3 - 4 carrots cut in small pieces
1 stalk of celery cut in small pieces
1 tsp. salt
1 tsp. pepper
1 tsp. garlic powder

Put everything in a large stock pot and simmer for 3 - 4 hours. When all remaining meat slips off the bones set the stock pot off the heat and remove the bones. Let cool and strain through a colander and freeze liquid in old plastic butter tubs. You won't be committing a crime if you alter the seasoning to suit your own taste. I like to salt and pepper the strained vegetables and meat and have as a snack.

VEGETABLE SOUP

Ingredients:

    1 quart venison soup stock
    1 large onion cut in wedges
    1 stalk celery cut in 1" pieces
    6 - 8 carrots cut in 1" pieces
    4 - 6 red spuds cut in 2" chunks
    ¼ head of cabbage, diced up
    ¼ head of Napa cabbage, diced up
    1 medium onion, diced up
    Salt and pepper to taste/your favorite seasonings

Put all ingredients in a 12" DO and simmer over 10 - 12 briquets for 45 minutes. Add a handful of rotelli pasta or egg noodles 15 minutes before serving for a change of pace.

Serves 6 - 8

Cee Dub... preparing the vegetable soup for a hungry crew.
Mike Robertson Photo

FISH STOCK

When baking or poaching fish some homemade fish stock used as the cooking liquid will add extra flavor. Like any other stock it can be made ahead of time and frozen until your ready to use it.

I prefer to use crappie/bluegill or bass for my stock. When I catch a mess of crappie I'll keep 6 - 8 carcasses which I rinse well after filleting for my stock.

Ingredients:

2 - 3 quarts of water
1 tsp. salt
1 tsp. lemon pepper
½ cup white wine vinegar
½ cup sauvingon blanc (optional)
1 medium onion finely diced
2 carrots sliced thin
2 stalks of celery finely minced
6 peppercorns
2 whole cloves
2 whole allspice
3 - 4 bay leaves
6 sprigs of fresh parsley finely minced
6 - 8 fish carcasses

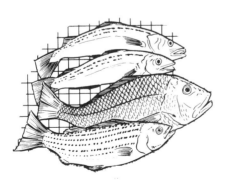

Bring the water to a boil in a large stock pot. Add all ingredients and simmer for 15 - 20 minutes. Set aside to cool. Strain and store in tupperware containers.

_____CHICKEN/POULTRY STOCK _____

Besides being one of the old stand by remedies for a cold, chicken stock has multiple uses in cooking for the well as well. Any time you roast a chicken or turkey, save the left over carcass for poultry stock. Just to keep from confusing avian taxonomists, stock made from any of the following will be referred to as chicken stock. (Chicken, turkey, pheasant, chuckar, blue grouse etc.) Besides using the carcass of a roasted bird you've carved the meat off of, you can start with the fresh legs, wings or backs of uncooked birds just as easily.

Ingredients:

2   bird carcasses
1   medium onion diced in ¼" chunks
3   stalks of celery sliced ½" thick
3   good sized carrots cut like the celery
½   cup chopped fresh parsley
2 - 3 quarts of water
Salt and pepper

Put all the ingredients in a stock pot and simmer over low heat for a couple of hours or until the meat easily falls off the bones. Cool for awhile then strain through a colander. For stock, reserve the broth and refrigerate or freeze for later use.I like to make **CREAM OF CHICKEN SOUP** and you need just a couple of more ingredients.

2 - 3 Tbsp. cornstarch
½ cup cream or 1 cup unsweetened
    condensed milk

After straining the stock, remove all the bones and chop the larger pieces of meat into ¼" chunks. Add the vegetables and chopped meat back to the stock. Bring to a simmer over low heat for about 10 minutes. Slowly add the cream or unsweetened condensed milk while you mix well with a wire whisk. Mix the cornstarch and ½ cup cold water. Add this to the soup a little at a time until it thickens to suit you. Make sure you continue to stir well with your wire whisk while adding the cornstarch. For a little variety, add a cup of broccoli florets and/or a handful of mushrooms.

CHICKEN AND NOODLE ⸻ JACK CHEESE CASSEROLE ⸻

Ingredients:

1   Batch of chicken stock
1   12 oz. package of egg noodles
2   roasted chicken breasts cut into ½" chunks (young of the year blue grouse is best)
1   medium yellow onion diced up
1   batch of home made Jack Cheese Sauce (See Sauce recipes)
1   can of black olives pitted and sliced
1   cup of fresh sliced mushrooms or two 4 oz. cans drained
Salt/pepper plus whatever other seasonings you might like (Try a teaspoon of caraway seed for a different zest.)

Pour your batch of chicken stock into a 12" DO and bring to a boil over a camp stove or 10 -12 charcoal briquets. Add the egg noodles and cook until about half done. Drain ½ of the remaining liquid off and reserve for another recipe. Stir the chicken chunks, onion, cheese sauce, and most of the black olives and mushrooms into the noodles. Set in the fire pan over 6 - 8 briquets and put about 20 on the top. Check after 15 - 20 minutes. Add more chicken stock, white wine, or water if needed. Bake for 30 - 40 minutes and garnish with the remaining olives and mushrooms just before you serve.

Serves about 6

TRISH'S FIRST NIGHT
——— at TALMAKS' SOUP ———

Patricia "Trish" Robertson, a Master's Degree, Licensed Professional Counselor, uses this great soup recipe in camp the first night when she conducts her "Women in the Wilderness" retreat programs. It's great and the final dish tastes like it took hours to put together.

Ingredients:

9 oz. pkg. Green Giant® Harvest Fresh Frozen Cut
    Broccoli, thawed before preparation.
6 cups water
3 cans,10 ¾ oz. condensed chicken broth
1 can, 10 ¾ oz. cream of chicken soup
2 cups cubed precooked chicken
1 cup chopped onions
Baby carrots - small package
2 cloves garlic
½ cup dry vermouth or water
½ Tsp. basil
½ Tsp. oregano
1 package, 7 oz. cheese tortellini
Grated parmesan cheese

Bring all ingredients, except tortellini and broccoli, to boil.

Add tortellini and simmer uncovered for 30 minutes. Add broccoli and simmer an additional 10 minutes. Serve with parmesan cheese to taste.

___ BASCO'S TERIYAKI MARINADE ___

Ingredients:

1 12 oz. bottle of soy sauce
½ cup brown sugar
1 cup water
6 cloves of garlic minced fine
2 Tbsp. finely minced fresh ginger

Place all ingredients in a sauce pan and bring to a boil. Allow to simmer for 5 - 10 minutes. Cool and store in refrigerator. Marinate any red meat or chicken for 1 - 2 hours prior to cooking.

Dave McGonigal
Game Warden, IDF&G
Boise, ID

BERGMAN'S WORLD CLASS MEAT MARINADE

Ingredients:

2 cups red wine vinegar
2 cups soy sauce, Kikkomans®
1 tsp. each of chopped parsley, thyme,
    oregano, basil, tarragon and rosemary.

Mix all ingredients and allow to blend (can be made in advance and stored in a jar). Enough for four pounds of meat (cubed or steaks), which should be marinated for at least one hour prior to preparation.
Great for "Cubed Elk Kabobs"

Harold Bergman
Fish Biologist
University of Wyoming

QUICK MEAT MARINADE

Drain the liquid from 3 - 4 small jars of marinated artichoke hearts. Put liquid in a glass jar and add 5 - 6 pressed or finely minced cloves of garlic. Use immediately or even better make it up a couple of days ahead and just leave it in the fridge. To make a small amount of marinade go farther, place your meat and marinade in a zip lock type freezer bag and roll it up to remove the excess air before you fasten the bag.

CEE DUB'S ITALIAN RED SAUCE

Ingredients:

1   28 oz. can of tomato sauce (homemade tomato
     sauce is even better if you have it)
½   cup burgundy wine
2 - 3 Tbsp. of olive oil
3 - 4   cloves of garlic pressed or minced
1   15 oz. can of tomatoes (whole, sliced,or diced -
     your choice)
1   15 oz. can of tomato paste
1   medium onion, diced into ½" pieces
4 - 5 Tbsp. of fresh chopped chives
Italian Seasoning. (If you can get fresh herbs such
     as marjoram, basil, sage, rosemary, oregano, and
     thyme, it's even better)

In a sauce pan large enough to hold it all, saute the garlic in the olive oil for 2 - 3 minutes. Add the remaining ingredients except for your seasonings and stir with a wire whisk until well mixed. If you use the dried Italian Seasoning, mix in 2 - 3 tablespoons and let simmer for about an hour. If you use fresh herbs, finely mince 1 - 2 tablespoons of your herbs and stir them into the sauce. A few minutes before serving, add the chopped chives. Simmer to the desired thickness or if you're in a hurry add an 8 oz. can of tomato paste. Thin with water or wine if needed.

BEER BATTER

Being more health conscious these days, I don't deep fry as often, but when I do this batter is what I use.

Ingredients:

8 oz. beer
2 egg whites
flour
salt/pepper or your favorite seasoning mix

With a wire whisk beat egg whites and beer. Add flour a little at a time till it looks like you've got runny pancake batter. I use this for fish fillets and venison finger steaks. Your batter can be seasoned to reflect what you're cooking.

CAPTAIN BOB'S
TEMPURA BEER BATTER

Captain Bob and Nancy Taylor, Haines, Alaska

Ingredients:

1 cup flour
½ tsp. salt
1 tsp. baking powder
1 egg beaten
2 Tbsp. vegetable oil
¾ cup flat beer or ice water

Combine dry ingredients and mix in beaten egg and vegetable oil. Add beer or ice water a little at a time until smooth. Cover and refrigerate till cooking time. (2 hours or even over night). Excellent for fresh Halibut, Salmon or Walleye.

Captain Bob and Nancy provided this recipe to Dan Miller while camped along the Chilkat River, Alaska, after a successful day of Halibut fishing in 1989.

A SIMPLE SIDE DISH, JUST LIKE A SAUCE, CAN MAKE YOUR MEAL COMPLETE!

——— MARINATED VEGETABLES ———

4 stalks fresh broccoli, chopped
8 large fresh mushrooms, chopped
1 medium size green pepper, chopped
3 stalks celery, chopped (save leaves for garnish)
1 small head cauliflower, broken into florets
3 carrots, sliced

Combine all vegetables and toss lightly.

¾ cup sugar
2 tsp. dry mustard
1 tsp. salt
²/₃ cup vinegar
1½ cup vegetable oil
1 small onion, quartered
2 Tbsp. poppy seed
Cherry tomatoes

Combine remaining ingredients, except cherry tomatoes, in blender, mix well and pour over vegetables. Garnish with celery leaves and cherry tomatoes. Chill at least 3 hours. Serves 10-12

————— RAINBOW RICE —————

1 bag of pre-measured rice, or rice for a serving of 4,
        prepared ahead of time
2 Tbsp. salad oil
1 can black olives, sliced
1 red pepper, sliced and diced
1 green pepper, sliced and diced
1 purple onion, sliced and diced
2 roma tomatoes, sliced and diced
Seasoned rice vinegar
Olive oil

Prepare rice with salad oil. Rinse thoroughly in a strainer to prevent clumping, and cool. In a large bowl, place cooled rice. Fold in olives, red and green peppers, onions, and tomatoes. Dress with the seasoned rice vinegar and olive oil.

CORNSTARCH GRAVY

I use cornstarch as a thickener when my meat has been cooked in a liquid. For example, when you make "Elk Rosemary," page 93, set the roast aside and spoon the vegetables into another pot and make your gravy in the DO you cooked the roast in. If desired, you can also just pour off excess liquid from a recipe and use it for your gravy base. To avoid lumpy gravy, mix the cornstarch in cold water before you add it to the pan drippings. I use a heaping tablespoon of cornstarch to about a quarter cup of cold water. Make sure your pan drippings are just simmering as you slowly add the cornstarch/cold water mix. Stir constantly until all the cornstarch has been added.

SAUSAGE GRAVY

When cooking for a bunch of hungry hunters, few breakfasts will stick to their ribs like sausage and gravy. If you baked an extra bunch of biscuits for supper it makes a quick and filling plate of grub before they head up the hill.

Ingredients:

1 lb. game or pork sausage	⅓ Cup flour
1 qt. milk	salt/pepper/seasonings

Brown the sausage in your DO until most of it is getting crispy. Add the flour and stir for 3 - 4 minutes until the grease is absorbed and the larger chunks of sausage covered with flour. Some folks like to make their gravy with seasoned flour. i.e. adding such things as paprika, season salt, garlic salt etc. to the flour before it's added to the DO. Have the DO setting over only 6 - 8 briquets. Any more and you risk burning or scorching the gravy. Add the milk, a little at a time, stirring constantly. After adding milk, let the gravy bubble to gauge how thick it is. Continue to add milk and stir until the desired consistency is achieved. The two most important things to remember are to use just enough grease so all your flour is absorbed and to stir constantly.

QUICK CAMP WHITE SAUCE and BASIC BROWN SAUCE
_____ with VARIATIONS _____

Call it sly, capricious, or just plain devil may care, but one of the sublime joys of being a good camp cook is to horn swoggle a "Pilgrim" who may be experiencing the outdoors for the first time. They find it tough to comprehend gourmet meals cooked under what they consider primitive conditions. In their minds they equate exotic foreign sounding dishes and recipes with their more familiar concrete jungle. Thank the "Great Camp Cook In the Sky" for the printing press. Otherwise self respecting practitioners of camp cooking would be forced to venture into such jungles just to graduate beyond the "Meat & Taters" stage! If you, like me, delight in seeing such awe in a Pilgrim's eyes, read on.

Ingredients:

4   Tbsp. margarine or butter
4   Tbsp. flour
2   cups water, white wine, chicken stock, or milk

Set a 10" DO over 6 - 8 briquets or on your camp stove on low heat. Melt the butter, then add the liquid and the flour, stir for 3 - 4 minutes with a fork or wire whisk. All you have to do to change this to a Basic Brown Sauce is use beef stock, venison stock, and a dash of burgundy wine. Basic sauces don't amount to much, but what you can do to them, will in the words of someone older than myself, "knock their socks off"! Use these variations to top main dishes, dress pasta, dress vegetables, or add to a casserole. If you've been paying attention you'll also recognize this as the foundation for a basic cheese sauce. Be creative and have fun.

SOME SUGGESTED VARIATIONS

For variety try adding one of these to your sauce.

Saute a couple of cloves of garlic and a tablespoon of fresh basil in a tablespoon of butter.

Saute 3 - 4 green onions including the tops, a small leek, or a couple of shallots.

Saute a cup of mushrooms with or without garlic.

Stir in two tablespoons prepared horseradish.

Add a couple of tablespoons of deli or Dijon mustard to accent a pork dish.

Two tablespoons each of ketchup, prepared horseradish and a dash of Tabasco® or other hot sauce when cooled makes a passable cocktail sauce.

Words of Wisdom

If at all possible, pack a couple of stainless steel thermos bottles. Especially in hunting camp, the cook will be less surly if someone makes a pot of coffee the evening before and fills a thermos to set with a cup next to his bunk. On the trail or on a raft trip, a thermos of hot chocolate or soup made at breakfast can be the first line of defense against hypothermia should someone get tossed out of a raft, or a sudden thunderstorm catches someone without their rain gear on.

HOME MADE CHEESE SAUCE

Sometime when you've nothing better to do, take a trip down the aisle (of the grocery store of course) and make a list of all the ready made sauces, marinades, prepared mixes etc., etc. now available. Most are good and can put an extra spin on a meal or a recipe without going to the trouble of making it at home from scratch. On the other hand though, nothing ever tastes quite as good as home-made!

Most of us, when we head for camp, throw in a couple of cans of cheese soup in case we need cheese sauce for a recipe. Some day when the weather keeps you in the cook tent, try making this for a real homemade taste.

Ingredients:

4 Tbsp. of margarine or butter
4 Tbsp. flour
2 cups milk
1+ cup grated cheese *
season to taste **

Set a 10" DO over 4 - 6 briquets and let the butter melt. Stir with a wire whisk and add your flour a little at a time. Keep stirring as you add the milk slowly. If it appears too hot remove a couple of briquets. When you get a nice smooth consistency, add the cheese and stir until it melts. Continue to stir over low heat to further reduce it if you want a thicker sauce. Makes 2 - 3 cups.

*   For variety try different types of cheese–i.e. Jalapeno Jack cheese for a Mexican dish, Swiss cheese for a lighter sauce, etc.

** Since most cheese has plenty of salt already I don't add any extra. Don't be afraid to mince up fresh herbs such as parsley, chives, or dill for different flavors or color. Also, I like to season mine with paprika or lemon pepper.

Vegetables
in Camp

POTATOES
aka
———— TATERS, SPUDS ————

Though someone, somewhere other than in Idaho, coined the phrase, "meat and potatoes", growing up in SE Idaho pretty much guaranteed one saw plenty of "taters" at meal time. Being a native Idahoan who happened to be born on the same day Idaho gained statehood, I'm duty bound to include a special section on spuds.(Actually I entered the scene sixty years after statehood).

Besides having eaten enough spuds in my life to say I've done my share to make "Idaho Famous", as a kid growing up I worked on several large potato farms. After graduating from college (as I related earlier in this book), I spent some time driving truck, long haul for my Uncle Harold. While doing so, I continued to do my part to make "Idaho Famous" by hauling 20 ton loads of spuds to areas not known for their tuber production!

In camp or in the kitchen, spuds are considered a staple world wide. The list of things spuds don't go well with is so short I'm not going to bother. Conversely the list they do go with is so long it would be prohibitive to list here. Besides having countless uses as a side dish, or as an ingredient in various recipes, spuds make great menu extenders. On those occasions when company comes unexpectedly, or your brother-in-law, without your knowledge, invites all of his in-laws to your deer camp, an extra sack of taters cooked any way you want will at least get you through meal time.

My dad, who spent more time than he cares to remember on KP duty in the army, could easily write a book just on peeling potatoes. However, the folks who count calories, grams of fat, and list all the nutrients in our chow tell us we're short changing ourselves nutritionally by peeling our taters. As camp cooks, anything which saves time fixing a meal means a little more time to spend fishing before heading back to camp to cook! Unless I'm making mashed pota-

172

toes for a formal dinner (which is rare) I save the hassle.

Fixed fancy or simple, spuds should be a staple in your grub box. I prefer fresh potatoes over all the other ways one finds them packaged in stores. However you fix them, always plan for seconds all the way around.

QUICK FRIED TATERS

Ingredients:

2 - 3 lbs. of spuds diced in ¼" - ½"
2 - 3 Tbsp. olive or vegetable oil
1 large onion diced
Salt and pepper or season to taste

Set a 12" DO on your camp stove over medium heat or in the firepan with 14 - 16 briquets underneath. Cut the spuds up while the oil heats up the DO. Add the spuds and turn every 2 - 3 minutes once they start to get crispy. I add my diced onion when spuds are about half done. Cook till done and top with grated cheese for a treat.
Serves 4 - 6

BAKED SPUDS —RIVER STYLE

Ingredients:

6 - 8 Idaho potatoes, washed and brushed
    with shortening
Enough small cleaned pebbles ¾ - 1" in diameter to
    keep potatoes from touching bottom of the
    Dutch oven.

Cover pebbles with water (one inch in bottom of Dutch oven). Place potatoes on the pebbles. Cover and place 6 - 8 briquets on top and 8 - 10 briquets on bottom. Bake one hour and serve. You can roast fresh ears of corn the same way, but decrease the cooking time by 40 minutes.

SPUDS and ONIONS AU GRATIN

Ingredients:

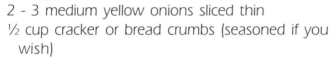

2 - 3 lbs. of russet spuds sliced
   as thin as you can
2 - 3 Tbsp. melted butter or
   margarine
2 - 3 medium yellow onions sliced thin
½ cup cracker or bread crumbs (seasoned if you
   wish)
1 cup grated cheddar cheese
1 can, 15 oz. of cheese soup
¼ cup milk
Salt and pepper or seasoning to taste

Take a paper towel and wipe a 12" DO with a little olive
or vegetable oil. Layer the spuds in the DO and brush
each layer with the melted margarine and a little seasoning. Then put in a layer of onions and keep layering spuds
brushed with butter till you've used all your spuds and
onions. Thin the soup with a little milk and pour over the
top. Sprinkle the bread or cracker crumbs over and add
any additional seasoning. Set the Dutch in the firepan
with 4 - 6 briquets underneath and 16 - 18 on the top.
Bake for 40 - 45 minutes. Remove the DO from the firepan
and sprinkle the grated cheese over the top
and let set for 5 minutes or so before
serving.

Serves 6 - 8

BREAKFAST TATERS

If you've ever cooked for a bunch of elk hunters you already know they hate to wait for breakfast. With miles to ride or hike before dawn, tempers rapidly degrade when breakfast is late. To speed things up in the morning, bake a bunch of extra spuds the night before.

Ingredients:

6 - 8 Baked potatoes cut in 1" pieces
2 medium onions, diced up
2 - 3 Tbsp. olive or vegetable oil
Salt/pepper or your favorite seasoning

Since I'm always in a hurry in elk camp, I set my DO on the propane cook stove on low to medium heat. I let the oil heat up for 2 - 3 minutes then add my spuds and onions. Since elk hunters tend to be solitary by nature during the day, I usually apply a liberal dose of garlic salt and or garlic pepper just before I serve. These spuds only take about 10 minutes to prepare and cook. If you happen to have a little grated cheese handy, sprinkle some over the top just before you serve.

Serves 4 - 6

Words of Wisdom

Always pack as good a first aid kit as weight
and space will allow! Whether your car camping,
horse packing or on a raft trip make sure the first aid kit is readily accessible.

Be concerned with safety in all aspects of outdoor recreation. I always try to have contingency plans for any trip should someone get sick, injured, or severe weather disrupts original plans.

HOME MADE HASH

More than one hunting camp recipe has been the result of the cook getting bored and throwing all the leftovers together. So was born this recipe for hash.

Ingredients:
2   cups of finely diced leftover elk roast
3   baked potatoes diced into ½" cubes
1   medium onion diced fine
1   Tbsp. olive oil
1   cup venison or beef stock (Or 1 bouillon cube dissolved in a cup of water)
Salt/pepper or whatever other seasonings you prefer

Saute the onion until it's soft, then add all the remaining ingredients. Stir to mix and simmer for 15 - 20 minutes until most of the liquid has been absorbed or reduced. If possible, make it the night before and just reheat for breakfast.

Scramble up a dozen eggs in another Dutch and serve the hash as a side dish.

HOME MADE HASH AND WIDE EYES

Try this some morning when you have the time to start a little charcoal or use a shovel full of coals from the camp fire.

Ingredients:
1   batch of home made hash
6   eggs
Salt/pepper (A dose of Tabasco® Sauce works too)

Melt just a dab of butter or margarine in a 12" Dutch. Spoon in the hash and spread it evenly in the DO. Set the DO in a fire pan with about five briquets underneath and cook uncovered just until the hash starts to bubble. While the hash is heating, shovel the lid full of coals from the camp fire, or place 20 - 25 briquets on the lid. Take a coffee cup and press into the hash to make a nest of sorts. Break an egg into each nest then put the lid on the DO for about 6 - 8 minutes. When you take the lid off it looks like a "Wide Eyed Monster" of sorts.
Serves 3

───────────Words of Wisdom ───────────

An old outfitter I met while trapping grizzlies for the Park Service in the 1970's used a unique method to discourage bears from hanging around his camps. He'd scrounge nearly used aerosol cans of hair spray from his wife and daughters and take them to camp. If a bear started hanging around camp he'd smear the hair spray cans with a little bacon grease and set them a couple of hundred yards outside of camp on the ground. As he put it, "about the time the old bear crunched down on a can of hair spray, things started to happen purty fast!" He said his wilderness "mine field" of bacon scented aerosol cans quickly provided bears an advanced degree in "Avoidance!" A word of caution though, bears are like mothers in-laws; don't make them mad what ever you do!

"NO NAME CREEK"
BAKED BEANS

Often times recipes are born of necessity or thrown together out of what ever the cook can find left in the grub
box. So was born this recipe in a camp on "No Name Creek"
the fall of 1991.

Right now you're thinking this "No Name Creek" doesn't
exist and I'm just tryin' to protect a honey hole for elk hunting. Wrong! Look real close at a map of Chamberlain Basin in
Central Idaho, and you'll find the real "No Name Creek"
about a thirty minute horseback ride from Chamberlain
Airstrip.

I'd been assigned a two week hitch in Chamberlain as part
of an emphasized enforcement effort in the back country. I,
along with several others, rode and flew into Chamberlain to
relieve guys who'd been in since before the back country elk
hunt opened. Don Wright drew the duty of camp cook for
the first crew and I drew KP for the second group. Our tours
over-lapped a day; so Don and I combined our talents for
dinner. To this day neither of us remembers the main course
that night. Since my grub order wouldn't arrive till the next
day, we made do with what Don had on hand.

Looking in the grub box it appeared our choices for a
vegetable included kidney beans, black eyed peas, black
beans, navy beans, pinto beans, or pork and beans. With not
enough of any one kind to go around we had no choice but
to throw them all together. Looking at the ingredient list,
you'll see that lacking a real kitchen sink to throw in, we just
cleaned out the grub box.

Since then, I've served this recipe to several hundred
people, but I don't think it ever tasted quite as good as that
first night. I chalk it up to ambiance. Folks talk about how the
proper ambiance will make a good meal great. Only pilgrims
wouldn't classify the smell of wood smoke and dinner music
provided by horse bells as ambiance! Anyway...these beans
will provide their own ambiance.

"NO NAME CREEK" BAKED BEANS

Ingredients: For a 12" DO
I triple this for my 16" DO.

1 15 oz. can each of whatever different kinds of
beans you can lay your hands on.
1 large onion diced
½ cup molasses
Salt, pepper, garlic powder, dry mustard
A-1 Steak Sauce®, horseradish, ketchup
Worcestershire Sauce , etc.

Place first three ingredients in DO and add whatever amounts
you want of remaining ingredients. Don't hesitate to add any
other ingredients laying at the bottom of your grub box! If
you lack ambiance when served, just wait 3 to 4 hours!

Serves 10 - 12

_____ Words of Wisdom _____

If taking pre-packaged food to camp,
be sure you pack any extra ingredients
called for on the package, i.e. oil and
eggs for cake mixes.

When possible, pack dry goods in zip-lock bags to save
space. Keep a magic marker in your camp box to label
left overs.

A roll of heavy duty aluminum foil in the grub box always
seems to get used.

Short cuts in planning and preparations invariably lead to
short tempers amongst the campers.

MIXED ITALIAN VEGETABLES

Ingredients:
1 - 2 small zucchini squash
1 - 2 small yellow summer squash
1 large green bell pepper
1 large sweet red bell pepper
1 large yellow bell pepper
1 large purple onion
1 cup water or white cooking wine
Italian seasoning

Slice all ingredients and place in a 12" DO. Sprinkle with Italian Seasoning. If available use fresh herbs instead. Oregano, thyme, sage, rosemary, basil, or marjoram will work. Use all of them or any three for an Italian flavor.

Add water or wine and steam for about 15 minutes with 10 - 15 coals on the bottom. Serves 6 - 8.

——CEE DUB'S FANCY VEGGIES——

Ingredients:
2 lbs. young tender carrots - scrubbed &
    sliced ½ inch thick
2 lbs. new red potatoes scrubbed
1 lb. white pearl onions peeled
¼ - ⅓ lb. butter
3 - 4 cloves garlic minced or pressed
2 cups chablis or sauvignon blanc wine
1 cup fresh parsley - finely minced

Place potatoes, carrots, and onions in 12" DO. Add the wine and let steam for about 30 minutes. Melt the butter and add the garlic. When the veggies have steamed, drain off the liquid and pour butter and garlic over them. Sprinkle with the parsley and toss before serving.

Serves 8 - 10

EASY ORIENTAL VEGETABLES

Ingredients:
2 cans 15 oz. each of mixed Oriental Vegetables (drained)
1 8 oz. can of water chestnuts (drained)
4 cloves of garlic pressed or minced
1 Tbsp. fresh minced ginger is optional
2 Tbsp. olive oil
1 Tsp. of Chinese Five Spice
2 Tbsp. of soy sauce

Saute the garlic and ginger in olive oil until garlic is golden brown in a 10" DO. Add all remaining ingredients and stir to mix. Cook over 8 - 10 briquets for 8 - 10 minutes stirring frequently.   Serves 6 - 8

QUICK FRESH MIXED VEGGIES

Ingredients:
1 lb. cauliflower florets
1 lb. carrots cut diagonally in ½" slices
1 lb. broccoli florets
1 small purple onion diced
¾ Cup water, dry white wine, or chicken stock
Salt/pepper or use Mrs. Dash's® Salt Free and Extra Spicy Seasoning for a different taste

Combine all the ingredients in a 12" DO and set in the firepan over 12 - 14 briquets. Watch closely and remove from the firepan 2 - 3 minutes after you first see steam escaping.   Serves 6 - 8

BAKED CORN CASSEROLE

Ingredients:
1 can whole kernel corn - don't drain
1 can creamed corn
1 cup sour cream
¼ cup butter melted
1 small package corn muffin mix

Place in greased dutch or casserole pan.
Bake at 350° for 60 minutes.

Julie Pedersen, Hamilton, MT

MIDDLE FORK MEXICAN CORN

One night while camped near the mouth of Little Aparejo Creek on the Middle Fork of Salmon River another officer and I dug the fixin's for this out of our kitchen box to go along with some enchiladas. Try this on "Mexican Night" or just to add different flavor and/or color to this staple of back country grub boxes.

Ingredients:
2 15 oz. cans of corn
1 4 oz. bottle of pimentos drained and diced
1 4 oz. can of green chilies drained and diced
1 Tsp. of cumin
Salt/pepper to taste

Dump everything into a 10" Dutch and set it over the coals of a campfire until it boils. In 10 minutes you're ready to serve.
Serves 6 - 8

QUICK AND SIMPLE GREEN BEANS
—————— (FANCY STYLE) ——————

Ingredients:

4   left over strips of bacon from breakfast
2   15 oz. cans of french cut green beans
1   can of cream of mushroom soup
Lemon pepper to taste, or whatever else you like
    on your green beans

Crumble up the leftover bacon then mix all ingredients in a 10" DO.

Set your DO in the firepan over 8 - 10 briquets and bring to a boil. This takes about 10 minutes and believe me they'll go back for more of these.   Serves 6 - 8

————— RANCH VEGGIES —————

Ingredients:

1   cup carrots scrubbed and cut in ½" slices
2   cup broccoli florets
2   cup cauliflower florets
1   green bell pepper cut in ½" strips
½   medium purple onion diced up
1   sweet red bell pepper cut in ½" strips
¾   cup water or white wine
1   package dry ranch salad dressing mix

Put all the ingredients into a 12" Dutch and steam for about 10 - 15 minutes over 10 - 12 briquets. While the veggies steam mix the ranch dressing according to package directions. Drain any excess liquid off and pour dressing over the veggies. Toss to mix and garnish with croutons, if you have them.   Serves 6 - 8

CAULIFLOWER and BROCCOLI
—with PEPPER CHEESE SAUCE—

Ingredients:

3 cups cauliflower florets
3 cups broccoli florets
1 cup white wine or water
1 can cheddar cheese soup
Coarse ground pepper

Have 10 - 12 briquets ready. Put the cauliflower and broccoli florets in a DO and stir to mix them. Add ¾ of the cooking liquid and set over the briquets for 8 - 10 minutes or until you notice steam escaping. While you're waiting for them to steam, thin the cheese soup with your remaining liquid. Once the vegetables begin to steam remove the lid and pour in the cheese soup. Sprinkle with coarse ground pepper to taste. You shouldn't need any salt as the store bought soup usually has plenty.   Serves 6 - 8

STEAMED BROCCOLI with DILL

Ingredients:

8 cups broccoli florets
2 - 3 Tbsp. margarine or butter
1 Tbsp. dill (The store bought type)
½ cup dry white wine or water
Juice from half a lemon (Can use bottled lemon juice)

Put the broccoli and cooking liquid in a 12" DO and steam for about 8 minutes over 10 - 12 briquets. While waiting for the broccoli, melt the butter then add lemon juice to butter. Stir to mix. When the broccoli has steamed, drain any liquid off then pour the butter and dill mixture over the top. Toss to mix before serving. This goes especially well with most fish dishes.   Serves 6 - 8

BOB'S SMOTHERED BROCCOLI

Ingredients:
2 pkgs. (10 oz.) frozen chopped broccoli, thawed
   or 1 ½ pounds fresh broccoli,   chopped
1 16 oz. carton cottage cheese
½ pound cheddar cheese, shredded
¼ pound butter cubed
5 Tbsp. flour
1 Tbsp. seasoned pepper

Topping:
Paprika
3 slices bread torn into small pieces
¼ pound butter, melted

Combine broccoli with ingredients and mix well. Place into a greased dutch. For the topping, take the bread pieces and soak them in the melted butter—sprinkle them evenly over the top of the broccoli mixture. Shake paprika over top. Cover the Dutch and bake for 1 hour at 350° .

Bob Jackson, Nampa, Idaho

____SUMMER ITALIAN VEGGIES____

Ingredients:

2 cups sliced zucchini squash
2 cups sliced yellow crook neck squash
1 large purple onion sliced
1 sweet red bell pepper sliced in ½" strips
1 green bell pepper sliced in ½" strips
2 - 3 cloves of garlic pressed or finely minced
3 Tbsp. margarine or butter
¼ Cup Parmesan cheese
Italian Seasoning or a ½ tsp. each of minced
    fresh oregano, thyme, rosemary, basil, and sage.

Set a 12" DO over 10 - 12 briquets or on your camp stove
over medium heat. Saute the garlic in the margarine or butter
for 2 - 3 minutes. Add all the vegetables and fry for another
6 - 10 minutes. Sprinkle your seasoning on just the last
couple of minutes of cooking. Remove from the heat and
sprinkle the cheese over the top. Let set a few minutes with
the lid on then serve.   Serves 6 - 8

____BAKED ONIONS in a DUTCH __

Ingredients:

6 - 8 medium sized onions
4 Tbsp. olive oil
1 tsp. salt (to taste)
½ tsp. pepper to taste, white pepper, if you have it
2 cups white sauce (See page 168)
4 cups liquid - use your imagination
2 Tbsp. butter
½ cup grated cheese

Peel whole onions, boil them in liquid in a deep pan until
tender - drain and arrange in oiled Dutch. Add white sauce
and butter. Bake for about 15 minutes. Carefully lift lid , add
grated cheese, cover and let cheese melt.   Serves 6 - 8
Mike Robertson, Twin Falls, ID

Garlic & Her Poor Cousin "Onion"

As I look back on my childhood, I can't remember many dishes, other than desserts, in which onions were not used. To say I come from a long line of onion eaters would be a true statement. Grilled hamburgers at a Welch family reunion are a case in point. The sliced onions disappear at a much greater rate than do the pickles, lettuce, and tomatoes.

Our household was a traditional meat and potatoes place when dinner time rolled around. Besides his meat and taters, Dad always had a big chunk of raw onion on the side. It was only after I left home for college that I realized everyone's dad didn't eat a half a raw onion for supper every night. Dad never made the **Guinness Book of Records** for his onion consumption, but now I suspect that is only because they didn't keep such records back then.

Not only did Dad eat more than his share of onions, he had the reputation in the neighborhood of growing the hottest onions in the county. Even when a seed catalog touted some variety as "very mild", Dad could somehow grow these onions so hot they couldn't be entered into interstate commerce without a "hazardous materials permit".

My guess is, some day, a guru researcher will identify a gene proving this love affair with onions is an inherited trait. A day which all card carrying members of OLA* look forward to! In some circles, the stigma of onion addiction might be more socially acceptable when it's proven to have a genetic basis. Anyway, whatever the cause, onions are always on my grub list whether I'm cooking at home or in camp.

The other night I sat reading through my collection of cook books doing research for this book. As I skimmed various recipes something seemed to nag at the edge of my subconscious. Finally, it struck me. Recipe after recipe was calling for just one clove of garlic! Even if medical science did not extol the benefits of garlic, unless eaten raw, a single clove of garlic will not, and I repeat will not, contribute to garlic over load!

A case in point, a chili recipe which serves ten people calls for only a single clove of garlic. People who are compulsive measurers will most likely go through their entire life only using what garlic a recipe calls for. In my case, I operate under the philosophy of "if a lot does a good job, more does it better." I admit, some ingredients can be over done in fixing different dishes, but you might want to try doubling or trebling the amount called for. You'll be surprised how the flavor of dishes calling for garlic are enhanced when you increase the amount of garlic, without being over-powering.

These two members of the lily family are essentials when I'm putting together a menu. In a pinch, I've even used the tops of wild onions in lieu of chives in camp. A word of caution to "Pilgrims" though, any time you plan to use edible wild plants in camp or at home, invest in an edible plants book first. Another member of the lily family has the common name of "Death Camas"! That is one mistake folks in camp would prefer you avoid!

* OLA is the acronym for ONION LOVERS ANONYMOUS

GARLIC BUTTER

Ingredients:
1 lb. butter or margarine
(Even squeeze bottle margarine)
4 cloves of garlic minced or pressed*

If using butter or margarine set it out and let warm to room temperature. (Hot summer days excepted). If your butter or margarine is in a plastic tub that will do, if using ¼ lb. sticks place them in a bowl and stir with a spoon. Add the pressed garlic and mix well. Let set for an hour or so then spread on bread. Just a hint which might save you some heart ache and grief. Always label this so folks don't confuse it with regular butter. Take my word that using this on one's pan-cakes with maple syrup will not bring a smile to the face of a hungry elk hunter.

* I use one clove of garlic per ¼ lb. of butter. For real garlic lovers use "big" cloves.

BASIL/GARLIC BUTTER

Ingredients:

1 lb. butter or margarine
4 cloves of garlic finely diced or pressed
4 fresh basil leaves finely diced

Mix and label as above. Great on bread or as a dressing for pasta.

Make this only with fresh basil. The freeze dried store bought variety has all the taste of finely diced green cardboard!

HERB BUTTER

Ingredients:

1 lb. butter or margarine
Fresh herbs

Mix as directed in the recipe for basic garlic butter. I like to mix 2 - 3 herbs together to obtain different flavors just for a change of pace. Fresh herbs are preferred but you can use store bought in lieu of home grown. I use ½ teaspoon of fresh herbs minced as fine as you can. Use a little more if using store bought herbs per pound of butter. Typically fresh herbs will yield a stronger more pungent taste than will those found on the shelf of the grocery store. Combinations I use are as follows, or make up your own combinations:

Chopped chives and basil
Thyme, sage and celery seed
Rosemary and oregano

Cee Dub prepares an herbed butter to dress the vegetables.

Mike Robertson Photo

SUGAR AND SPICE AND ───OTHER THINGS NICE───

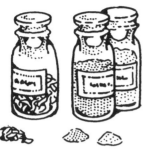

In the dim recesses of my mind, I vaguely remember a grade school teacher telling our class about wars being fought over spices. At the time it seemed rather foolish, but the teacher is supposed to be right. Anyway...as I've matured, my palate, along with various other body parts, now requires some assistance. Consequently, my use of spices and herbs has increased accordingly.

A couple of friends, for medical reasons, have had to suffer through a bland diet along with whatever ailed them. Both of them told me they didn't know what was worse. Being sick or eating "bland" food for weeks on end! Now, imagine an entire nation on a bland diet, and those long ago wars don't seem quite so unreasonable!

To a kid growing up on meat and taters in SE Idaho, exotic included anything other than salt and pepper. After twenty-five plus years of eating my own cookin', I've learned how merely varying the spices can turn a "ho hum plain jane dish" into something to brag about.

Spices and herbs are to cooking, as makeup is to women! Women utilize makeup to accent and highlight their natural beauty or to make the transformation from everyday to elegant. Herbs and spices perform the same function in the kitchen. Wise and judicious use of each will produce amazing results. Conversely, excessive use of either will ruin even a blind man's appetite!

Whether rafting, horsepacking, or car camping, my kitchen always contains a variety of spices. On a short trip and at home I use fresh herbs whenever possible. A huge difference exists between most store bought stuff and herbs fresh from the garden. Basil being a case in point. Dried basil from the supermarket more resembles green cardboard than anything else, when compared with fresh basil. When you pack your spices, start with salt and pepper as a minimum. After that the upper limit will be determined by personal choice and room in the chuck box.

I suppose there have been entire books written on just spices and herbs and their uses, but I confess I've never read any of them. However, I am a graduate of **T I T T & E***. The basic premise of **T I T T & E** is to expand upon seasoning called for in any given recipe. This philosophy can on occasion create truly phenomenal new dishes. Along the way many "trials and errors" result. "Trials" usually are edible depending on how hungry the diners, while "errors" may result in a trip to the vet for any neighborhood dog who might tip over your garbage can. On a more serious note though, don't be afraid to experiment.

In my case, because I never use exactly what the recipe calls for, variation to some degree always results. Besides the amount of seasoning, the timing of its' use may alter the finished product. For example, when making an Italian red sauce which should be simmered for a long time, I'll add a small amount of seasoning about 20 - 30 minutes prior to serving. When using fresh herbs this really enhances the flavor.

Whether you're an up and coming cook or someone like myself who falls in the category of "sagebrush chef", experimentation with spices and herbs should end only when six of your friends show up wearing clean shirts, bearing flowers, and wiping their eyes.

* THE INSTITUTE OF TRYING TRIAL & ERROR

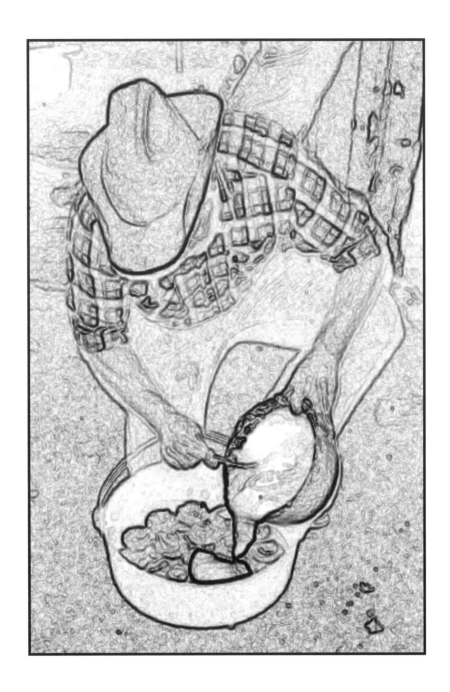

Snacks & Desserts

FANNY PACK SNACKS

When planning a trip of any sort don't forget some snacks to keep you going. Whether rafting, horse camping, hiking, fishing etc., some extra ready to eat grub when you're late getting into camp helps one's attitude. As with anything else though, convenience often translates into a bigger bill at the grocery store. If you doubt that statement go to the store and price some store bought jerky. Go home and with your calculator figure out the price per pound. You'll find you could eat rib eye steak three times a day for the same price. Make your own and you'll end up with better jerky at a fraction of the cost. I always make my own venison jerky, but you can use beef just as easily.

Over the last few years food dehydrators have been improved and price wise are very affordable. Just like making jerky, you can buy and dry a bushel of apples cheaper than you can buy a pound of dried apples off the grocery store shelf. Dried or dehydrated snacks take up less room, weigh less, and end up being more edible than fresh stuff after a couple of days in your saddle bags or day pack.

Cee Dub on the trail and you can bet he has his pack filled with snacks.   C.W. Welch Photo Collection

194

VENISON JERKY

I like jerky and have made my share over the years but a particular friend of mine is best described as a "jerky junky". Listening to Jon explain the nuances of his most recent recipe provokes images of a connoisseur speaking with an accent of a vintage French wine. While Jon continues his search for the perfect jerky recipe, I've settled on just one after trying many different ones.

Most recipes I've tried in the past ended up being too salty for my taste. "Salt to taste", I realize, is a relative term, but in using this recipe feel free to vary the amount according to your own taste.

Ingredients: Brine

¾ cup non-iodized salt
3 cups brown sugar
1 cup soy sauce
2 cups water
10 cloves of garlic, sliced thin

Combine all of the ingredients in a large pan and bring to a boil. Reduce heat and let simmer for about five minutes. Cool the brine to room temperature before using.

10 lbs. of beef, elk, deer, moose, antelope, etc.
coarse ground pepper

Trim all fat and as much connective tissue as you can off the meat. I cut my meat in strips 4 - 6 inches long, 1 - 2 inches wide, and about ½" thick. Place the meat in a large glass or crockery container and pour in the brine. Stir the meat and brine then set a plate with some weight on it to keep all the meat totally submerged in the brine. Refrigerate for 4 - 6 hours. Make sure you stir the meat 2 - 3 times while it's in the brine. Drain the brine off and reserve if you're going to make another batch within a week or so. Here is where you have several choices. I smoke my jerky over apple wood or mesquite. However, you can use a food dehydrator or even use your oven. When using an oven, I place the meat strips on cake racks with a cookie sheet for a drip pan on the oven rack underneath the meat.

I place the meat strips as close together as possible without them touching. At this time I sprinkle coarse pepper on to taste. How long it takes to dry will vary depending on the heat source, the thickness of your meat, and on personal preference. Some folks like it dry and others like it without all the moisture removed. If you're new to the game of making jerky, plan on checking every hour or so in order to get it just the way you like. What you don't end up eating right out of the smoker can be stored in the freezer or fridge. If you're going to keep it in the fridge, wrap it up in a piece of cheese cloth or in a brown paper grocery bag.

Note: If you're using a food dehydrator or oven add 1 tablespoon of liquid smoke to the brine for a "smoky flavor". Also, don't be afraid to experiment with other spices in the brine or sprinkled on prior to drying/smoking.

—— DUTCH OVEN NACHOS ——

Tortilla corn chips
Meat, if desired, such as shredded pork, or beef prepared
              Mexican style
Tomatoes, chopped
Onions, chopped
Cheese, grated
Olives, chopped
Sliced jalapeno peppers
Other toppings as desired
Sour cream, salsa, and/or guacamole

Place a tin foil plate in the bottom of a 16" Dutch oven. Put a layer of tortilla chips on the tin plate. Add the meat and other garnishments putting the cheese on top. Place the lid on the Dutch oven and heat for about 15 minutes or until the cheese melts. Use about 20-25 briquets on top of the Dutch oven to quickly heat the nachos. Slide tin plate of nachos from the Dutch oven. Serve with sides of sour cream, salsa, and/or guacamole as an added treat.

LISA MARTINY'S
——————QUICK FRUIT ROLLUPS——————

Ingredients:

1 dozen flour tortillas
1 15 oz. can pie filling of your choice

Warm each tortilla for a few seconds on each side. Spoon
1 to 2 tablespoons of pie filling onto the warm tortilla and roll
up and place in a buttered Dutch. Using the small "torts" you
can make 6 - 8 rollups in a 12" Dutch.

Bake with 4 - 5 briquets underneath and 4 - 18 on top for
about 10 minutes.Eat them hot for a great snack or dessert or
the next morning as a breakfast snack.

——————BLACKBERRY DUMP CAKE——————

Ingredients:

4 cups frozen blackberries, or other desired fruit
½ cup flour
1 white cake mix, with pudding included for moistness
1 20 oz. bottle of lemon-lime carbonated soda, such as 7-Up

Put fruit in the bottom of a 12" Dutch oven. Sprinkle flour over
the fruit for thickening. Sprinkle the dry cake mix over the fruit
and flour. Gently pour the carbonated soda over the cake mix.
Cover and bake using 4-6 briquets under the DO and 18-22 on
the lid of the DO to bake the cake. Baking should take about
35-45 minutes. You will know when it is done. The aroma of the
fruit and cake are unmistakable. Let stand to cool. Serve with
whipped cream, if desired.

CINDI'S APPLE CRISP

Ingredients: Fruit Mixture

6 cups pared apples sliced thin
¾ cup sugar
¼ cup flour
½ tsp. of nutmeg
½ tsp. of cinnamon
Dash of salt

Ingredients: Crumb mixture

1 cup of flour
¾ cup of rolled oats
1 cup of brown sugar
½ cup melted butter or margarine
1 tsp. cinnamon

Stir together the fruit mixture and spoon it into a 12" DO. Combine and mix all the ingredients for the crumb mixture. Spread/crumble this over the fruit filling. Set your DO in the firepan with 3 - 5 briquets underneath and 18 - 22 on the lid and bake for 45 - 50 minutes.

Serves 8
Contributed by Cindi A. Ferro

——— TRISH'S RHUBARB CRISP ———

Ingredients: Topping

¾ cup flour
¾ cup packed brown sugar
½ cup old-fashioned oats
½ tsp. ground cinnamon
¼ tsp. ground cloves
6 Tbsp. butter
½ cup chopped walnuts (optional)

For topping:

Mix first 5 ingredients. Rub in butter until mixture begins to clump together. Mix in nuts. Topping can be made ahead, chilled and taken to camp.

Ingredients: Filling

1½ lbs. rhubarb, cut into ½ inch pieces
   (about 7 - 8 cups)
3+ Tbsp. sugar
2 tsp. flour
½ tsp vanilla extract

For Filling:

Line dutch (10" or 12") with foil. Combine filling items in a large bowl and toss to coat. Transfer mixture into dutch oven.

Sprinkle topping evenly over fruit. Bake until fruit is tender or topping is crisp (about 45 minutes). Cool 20 minutes. Serve warm.

You can also bake it in a 8 x 8 x 2 glass baking dish in 400° F. oven for 45 minutes. Cool 20 minutes. Serve warm with vanilla ice cream or frozen yogurt.

RIVER RUNNIN'
BERRY and/or FRUIT COBBLER
_____ DESSERT in a DUTCH _____

This is an old "made in the kitchen" favorite that has been adapted to Dutch ovens. I've made this for crews of elk hunters and hungry river runners. After a long day of recreating and a big camp meal, the pilgrims you feed will think you have "made magic" with this dessert. You might want to double this recipe and make two. Depending upon number of hungry eaters and size of dutch used, it will be quickly devoured, and left overs (if any) become part of breakfast.

Ingredients:

1 to 3 cans of your favorite canned pie filling from
    blackberries to cherries to apples & peaches, or
    all of the above.
Pillsbury® pre-made pie crust
Canola or vegetable oil
1 cube butter (used with fruits, not berries)
1 cup brown sugar (used with fruits, not berries)
24 to 30 charcoal briquets
Dutch oven (I prefer the old 12" standby)

Line inside of Dutch with aluminum foil and coat with canola or vegetable oil. Don't use butter, it burns! Put berry filling directly in lined bottom of dutch. Add brown sugar and melted butter when using fruit fillings.

Cover ingredients with pre-made pie crust, piercing with fork in 10 - 12 places. Place covered Dutch over half of the hot coals, and put rest on top of Dutch lid. You can make it a "pie" by using a pie crust on the bottom then your filling. Crimp edges and pierce as above.
Cook slowly until filling is hot and crust is baked crisp on top. Serve up warm, but get out of the way of the crowd!

Serves 8 to 10 per dutch, or less depending upon how hungry everyone is.

_____ Words of Wisdom _____

In the summer make up your own freeze jugs for your coolers. I use plastic juice containers of one quart and one half gallon. Make up ice tea, powdered fruit drinks, and drinking water and fill jugs 2/3 full. Put them in the freezer and freeze. Pack your cooler with these instead of commercial blocks of ice to save space and money. In addition, beer in the can may be frozen and used in lieu of ice. Don't try it with near beer or soft drinks.

In the middle of the summer or on long trips, pack your coolers to be opened according to when you plan to use them. Stuff will stay frozen longer if you don't open them until you're ready. I tightly strap the lid down with a boat strap and then go around the lid with duct tape. It can add 3-4 days to how long you can keep stuff frozen.

REDHOT RHUBARB
UPSIDE DOWN CAKE - THE STORY

About the time I was born in 1950, the Idaho Deptartment of Fish and Game began to purchase homesteads in Idaho's back country. These homesteads dated from the early days of statehood. Over the years the hard scrabble homesteaders had eked out a living by raising stock, produce, hunting, fishing, trapping and occasional work for the US Forest Service. By the time WW II ended, it was just too tough to any longer make a living for most. With livestock removed, many of these places simply reverted to native vegetation. Some were leased by IDFG to outfitters as base camps and others used as patrol cabins by IDFG personnel.

"Western" best describes these old cabins after 70+ years of use. One such cabin at Cougar Creek on the Middle Fork of Salmon River became one of my "back country homes" while stationed at Challis 1978 - 1987. A couple of different years I even put in a small garden. The fire guard up stream six miles at Little Creek Guard Station would periodically irrigate it for me. I would put in some onions, radishes, carrots, and lettuce. Usually

Piero Piva relaxin' on the front porch of the Cougar Creek Cabin at Challis, Idaho.   C.W. Welch Photo Collection

the cottontail rabbits would leave just enough to make a garden fresh salad when I stopped on summer float patrols. I always put my garden back behind the house next to an old clump of rhubarb where some earlier inhabitant had gardened.

Another officer's sweet tooth provided the stimulus one night to make a dessert with rhubarb. We were in to clear brush and shovel out the irrigation ditch so we could try and rejuvenate part of the horse pasture. Our grub list was fairly simple, but the grub box in the cabin held a little extra stuff too. Necessity being the mother of invention to use an old cliche, gave rise to this recipe.

REDHOT RHUBARB UPSIDE DOWN CAKE - THE RECIPE

Ingredients:

4 cups of rhubarb washed and cut in 1" chunks
½ cup brown sugar
1 cup water
½ cup of cinnamon red hot candy
1 store bought cake mix
2 Tbsp. margarine

Put the first three ingredients in a 10" DO and simmer about 30 minutes. When the rhubarb is well cooked and starting to thicken, add the cinnamon red hots and stir until they're dissolved. Let the rhubarb/red hot mixture cool for a few minutes while you mix up your cake mix according to package directions. Next set your 12" DO in the firepan over 4 - 6 briquets and let your margarine melt. Take a spatula and make sure the melted margarine completely covers the bottom of the DO. Spoon the rhubarb into the DO and spread evenly. Then pour the cake mix over the rhubarb. Bake with 20 - 25 briquets on top until it smells done which is usually about 40 minutes.

A note when making upside down cake—if you have fruit juice left over from breakfast, add it to your cake mix in place of the water for a moister cake.

PINEAPPLE - APRICOT
____UPSIDE DOWN CAKE____

Ingredients:

¾ cup maple syrup
8 Tbsp. margarine

Place in 12" Dutch oven over 4 - 6 briquets and bring to boil. Boil for 3 - 4 minutes. Remove from heat.

1 can pineapple slices
1 can halved apricots

Arrange pineapple slices on bottom of Dutch oven with an apricot in the center of each slice. Cover fruit with the following cake batter.

8 Tbsp. shortening
1 ½ cup sugar
2 eggs
1 cup milk
2 cup flour
2 tsp. vanilla
2 Tbsp. baking powder

Cream shortening, add sugar and mix well. Add eggs and beat well. Mix baking powder with flour, add alternately with milk. Add vanilla. Beat well and spread over fruit. Bake in Dutch oven for 30 - 40 minutes or until toothpick comes clean. Use 5 briquets on bottom, 18 - 22 briquets on lid. At home, cut ingredients by ½ and bake in regular cake pan in a moderate oven for 30 minutes.

CINDI'S PINEAPPLE
———— UPSIDE DOWN CAKE ————

Ingredients:

1   8½ oz. can sliced pineapple rings,
    drain & reserve juice
1   yellow cake mix
2   Tbsp. butter or margarine
⅓   cup brown sugar
Maraschino cherries

Fix this in a 10" DO in camp or your 10" cast iron skillet at home.

Mix the cake mix according to package directions. Substitute the pineapple juice for the liquid called for in the mix directions. If you don't have enough juice, just add water to make up the difference.

While you're making up the cake batter, set your 10" DO in the firepan over 6 - 8 briquets and melt the margarine. When the margarine has melted, sprinkle in the brown sugar. Starting on the outside of the DO, place the pineapple rings all the way around with one in the center. Place a maraschino cherry in the center of each pineapple ring. Pour the cake batter over the pineapple rings.

Bake for 25 - 30 minutes with 14 - 16 briquets on top and three underneath. At home bake in a 350 degree oven for 25 - 30 minutes.

Invert DO over a serving plate immediately after removing the charcoal. Let cool for 10 minutes then serve.

Serves 6 - 8

Cindi A. Ferro

DAN MILLER'S
——— UPSIDE DOWN CAKE ———

Ingredients:

1 can pineapple rings in juice, save juice
½ cup brown sugar, packed
1 box yellow cake mix, Jiffy®
1 egg
1 cup milk
½ cup maraschino cherries
1 oz. cherry brandy

Line 10" Dutch with aluminum foil and grease the foil with Crisco® or a spray vegetable shortening

Arrange pineapple slices and cherries on bottom. Sprinkle brown sugar over slices and add a little juice and cherry brandy to make a thick syrup.

Mix cake mix as per instructions on box using egg and milk. Beat mixture and pour over pineapple/cherries.

Cover Dutch and bake at 350° until cake is lightly browned on top. (5 or 6 briquets on bottom, 18 - 22 briquets on lid.) Approximately 45 minutes.

Remove from heat and allow to cool slightly before flipping onto serving plate. Remove foil while warm and slice.

Serving idea: Cook gets to drink leftover brandy!

(Double recipe for 12" Dutch)

Dan Miller - 1989 Green River Trip

MCLAIN'S QUICK & EASY CAKE

Ingredients:

2 cups flour
1 cup sugar
2 eggs
2/3 cup vegetable oil
2 tsp. cinnamon
21 oz. can of fruit pie filling
    (peach or apple is good)
1½ tsp. baking soda

Mix all ingredients. Put into aluminum foil lined, ungreased Dutch and cook 40 - 50 minutes. Use 8 briquets on bottom. Cover loosely.

Mike McLain
Colorado Division of Wildlife

FRIED APPLES

Core and slice into ¼" wedges, unpeeled, firm apples (enough to fill a large skillet). Put enough shortening in skillet to cover the bottom. Add a bit of butter or margarine to enhance the flavor. Toss apples in pan until they are well coated and allow to cook, but not get mushy. Add brown or granulated sugar to taste and ½ cup maple syrup. After apples are cooked, sprinkle with cinnamon or cardamon. Great not only for dessert, but also with Camp Bread or as a side dish for baked ham.

Joyce Cowan
Hamilton, Montana

Good night...

Ellis
Pendergraft

Front and Back cover photography by Mike Robertson